INTERNATIONAL
TRAIN-FERRY WAGONS
in Colour
for the Modeller and Historian

David Ratcliffe

Ian Allan
PUBLISHING

First published 2009

ISBN 978 0 7110 3404 4

© David Ratcliffe 2009

Published by Ian Allan Publishing

an imprint of Ian Allan Publishing Ltd, Hersham,
Surrey, KT12 4RG
Printed in England by Ian Allan Printing Ltd,
Hersham, Surrey, KT12 4RG

Code: 0910/B

Visit the Ian Allan Publishing website at
www.ianallanpublishing.com

CONTENTS

Title page: Having arrived from Dunkerque, the
Nord Pas-de-Calais prepares to berth at Dover
in April 1995. On the left can be seen the
computer-controlled linkspan installed in 1987.
Using two shunting locomotives at Dover, the
ferry could be unloaded and reloaded with a full
complement of railway wagons in 45 minutes.

Right: The 120ft linkspan from Southampton
and the lifting gantry from Richborough were
reused at Harwich, where they remained from
1924 until the service ended in 1987. The
linkspan was double-track, matching that on the
stern of the ships, and to cater for the tidal range
could be raised or lowered to a maximum
gradient of 1 in 20, the control room for the
electrically-driven machinery being located in
the cabin on top of the gantry. With a brake van
as a reach wagon, a Class 31 propels vans and
tank wagons onto the ferry at Harwich one
evening in April 1978.
David Monk-Steel collection

INTRODUCTION

Internationally registered wagons, or ferry wagons as they were often known, have long been an interesting part of the railway scene given the wide variety of types that have visited Britain. As such they have always been a favourite of mine and the fact that they came from foreign lands and had made a sea crossing to get here only added to their appeal.

THE TRAIN FERRIES

The first train ferries began operating between Britain and the Continent towards the end of World War 1, sailings on the Southampton–Dieppe and Richborough–Calais routes carrying military supplies for the Western Front. Three 2,600-ton ships, prosaically named *Train Ferry No1*, *Train Ferry No2* and *Train Ferry No3*, were built for the first service from Southampton in 1917, and these were later purchased by the London & North Eastern Railway for its new commercial service between Harwich and Zeebrugge, which began on 26 April 1924. Run as a joint operation with the Belgian National Railway, two ships made up to six sailings a week in either direction, with the third on standby. The difficult economic circumstances at the end of the decade discouraged any further development, so it was not until October 1936 that the Southern Railway, in partnership with the Nord Railway in France, started its own service between Dover and Dunkerque with three new 2,900-ton vessels — the *Hampton Ferry*, the *Shepperton Ferry* and the *Twickenham Ferry*.

All sailings were suspended in September 1939 upon the outbreak of World War 2, the six ships being requisitioned by the Royal Navy for use as troop-carriers and as transports for army vehicles of every description. Unfortunately *Train Ferry No2* and *Train Ferry No3* were lost during the war, and when services were able to recommence in 1946 a new ship, the *Suffolk Ferry*, was built to join *Train Ferry No1*, now renamed the *Essex Ferry*, on the Harwich run. To cope with steadily increasing demand a further three ships, the *Norfolk Ferry*, a second *Essex Ferry* and the *Cambridge Ferry* were built between 1951 and 1963, the first *Essex Ferry* being withdrawn in 1957. In common with the original vessels all the new ships were stern loading with four tracks on their train deck merging into two to correspond with those on the linkspan. However, they were 39ft longer and could accommodate the equivalent of 24 British Rail long-wheelbase two-axle ferry vans. Normally three of the four ships would be in operation at any one time, each making a single round-trip every weekday.

In 1967 the *Norfolk Ferry* began operating a daily out and back service from Harwich to Dunkerque which required a modification to the vessel's stern to fit the train ferry berth at Dunkerque. Primarily intended for perishable traffic destined for the Midlands, North of England and Scotland this service fell victim to the recession of the early 1980s as BR not only withdrew from the Harwich–Dunkerque route, but also reduced its Harwich–Zeebrugge operation. From June 1980 the *Speedlink Vanguard*, a double-deck ferry taken on bareboat charter from Stena Line, replaced all the earlier ships at Harwich.

With space for 50 two-axle wagons it should have produced considerable savings, but it quickly became apparent that its proclaimed capacity was more theoretical than factual as the on-board inter-deck lift frequently malfunctioned. Furthermore only the upper-deck was suitable for stationing wagons loaded with dangerous goods and so the *Cambridge Ferry* had to be reinstated, making seven trips a fortnight.

By 1980 the Dover–Dunkerque route was in the hands of the 1951-built *St Germain* which could accommodate 25 two-axle wagons and the 1975-built *St Eloi* with space for 35 two-axle vehicles. Plying the much shorter sea route across the channel each ship made two round trips a day but three were possible at times of peak demand and therefore it was no surprise when the decision was made to withdraw the Harwich service completely at the end of January 1987 and concentrate all activity at Dover. As a stop-gap the *Cambridge Ferry* was adapted to provide additional capacity and took up sailings from Dover early in 1987 until all three ships were replaced on the Dover–Dunkerque route by a new vessel, the *Nord Pas-de-Calais*, in January 1988. Owned by SNCF and named after the region of France in which the port of Dunkerque is situated, the new ship could carry 30 bogie wagons on its six tracks with space available at the stern for the equivalent of four bogie wagons loaded with hazardous cargoes. With a top speed of 21 knots it could cross the Channel in under two hours and new berthing facilities were installed at both ends of the route whereby loading could take place whatever the state of the tide without the time-consuming practice of the ship having to enter a closed dock. As such the

Right: The timings of sailings at Harwich were still dependent to some degree on the tide, it being preferable to have the linkspan as level as possible, particularly when shunting bogie wagons on and off the ferry. In June 1978 a rake of three-door Cargowaggon vans and an Interfrigo van come off the ferry at Harwich. *David Monk-Steel collection*

Above: For safety reasons wagons loaded with dangerous goods were carried at the stern of the ship, where they were more accessible in case of fire. Two of Associated Octel's fleet of anti-knock tanks head for Zeebrugge aboard the second *Essex Ferry* in December 1979.

Left: As a matter of course all wagons would be chocked and chained down when making the crossing. A bogie Cargowaggon van and a VTG 'Arcton' tank are seen chained to the deck of the *Cambridge Ferry* on an inclement day in March 1982.

Nord Pas-de-Calais could make four round trips in a day if required although for most of the year the schedule called for three each weekday and two on Saturdays.

In 1983 70% of the wagons arriving in Britain loaded had returned empty to the Continent, and in addition to the investment in new equipment there was a drive to increase export tonnage so that by the early 1990s the figure had been reduced to less than 50%. In 1993 the *Nord Pas-de-Calais* handled approximately 20,000 incoming wagons carrying about 950,000 tonnes of freight but following the opening of the Channel Tunnel in June 1994 this gradually declined. The first regular wagonload service began running through the tunnel in December 1994, two more, between Wembley and Lille, being introduced in May 1995, but a limited quantity of conventional wagonload traffic, including all dangerous goods, remained with the train ferry until its final sailing from Dover on 22 December 1995.

OPERATIONS AT HARWICH AND DOVER

Most train-ferry traffic was moved by wagonload freight services and as the vast majority of the wagons were air-braked they fitted neatly into the Speedlink trunk network which BR developed in the 1970s. Wagons arriving at Harwich from Zeebrugge would be tripped from the train ferry terminal, situated at the very end of the Harwich branch near Harwich Town station, to the main yard adjacent to Parkeston Quay a mile or so to the west. Here they were checked and then marshalled into one of seven daily Speedlink departures which ran to Bescot, Doncaster, Mossend, Tees Yard, Temple Mills, Tinsley and Warrington. In 1985 a similar number of arrivals were due at Harwich by midday which gave staff ample time to check that the wagons' documentation was in order so that they could be shipped later that day either on the evening sailing of the *Cambridge Ferry* or the midnight departure of the *Speedlink Vanguard*. If all went to plan a wagon's

average journey time from its UK point of origin was three days to destinations in Belgium and the Netherlands, four to those in Germany and five to Austria and Switzerland. Similar operations took place at Dover, which until 1987 had concentrated on traffic with France, Spain and Italy, with direct Speedlinks running to Bescot, Mossend, Temple Mills, Tyne Yard and Willesden as well as a dedicated working to the Transfesa depot at Paddock Wood. From 1987 there was also a train to Warrington and two additional workings to Willesden.

The closure of Speedlink in July 1991 had only limited impact on the train ferry since obligations in the Channel Tunnel Treaty with France required international wagonload services to be retained and as a result BR's Railfreight Distribution sector had to introduce a slimmed-down dedicated network for this traffic. This involved five weekday trains from Dover, with departures at 01.20 and 04.05 to Willesden, 09.05 to Crewe, 17.05 to Bescot and 18.05 to

Cardiff, from where feeder services forwarded the wagons to their eventual destination.

The BR TOPS (Total Operations Processing System) computer generated a train list for every working, showing details of the locomotive and wagons in each train with their load, originating point and destination, although for wagons running to and from the Continent the relevant entry would show up as either 49421 (Harwich Train Ferry terminal) or 89691 (Dunkerque via Dover) rather than an actual location abroad. Nevertheless these documents were very useful in casting light on the various traffic flows and all references made in this book to ladings and workings have been drawn either from TOPS train lists, other BR documentation such as Lost Wagon Reports and Wagon Labels, Manchester Ship Canal Co Railway records or personal observation. Given the scope of the traffic the six train lists that follow cannot be said to be exhaustive, but hopefully they give something of the flavour of these services.

6S73 Dover–Mossend, 3 April 1979 (locomotive No 33 060)

Wagon number	Type	Load	Destination
87 0798 007-2	ICA	Latex	Pan Ocean Storage, Ellesmere Port (Eastham)
71 0285 807-0	ITX	Fruit	Ardwick West, Manchester
83 0888 801-5	IIB	Fruit	Ardwick West, Manchester
83 2147 136-7	ILB	Fruit	Ardwick West, Manchester
83 0888 893-2	IIB	Fruit	Spekeland Road, Liverpool
87 2141 033-8	ILX	Chipboard	Ardwick West, Manchester
70 2140 015-5	VIX	Chipboard	Ardwick West, Manchester
71 0284 617-4	ITX	Fruit	Ardwick West, Manchester
71 0285 670-2	ITX	Fruit	Ardwick West, Manchester
71 0284 831-1	ITX	Fruit	Glass Glover, Slateford
71 0284 681-0	ITX	Fruit	Glass Glover, Slateford
80 0299 029-7	IPB	Chipboard	Glasgow High Street
71 0285 868-2	ITX	Fruit	Glasgow High Street

Note: Fruit and vegetables in two-axle vans dominated the traffic passing through Dover at this date.

7M86 Harwich–Warrington, 30 September 1985 (locomotive No 37 104)

Wagon number	Type	Load	Destination
80 2140 103-7	IMB		English China Clays, Marsh Mills
80 2140 023-7	IMB		English China Clays, Marsh Mills
80 4141 501-1	IPB	Aluminium alkyl halides	Amoco, Milford Haven
88 2380 057-6	ILB	Detergent	Manchester International Freight Terminal
88 2380 065-9	ILB	Detergent	Manchester International Freight Terminal
88 2380 187-1	ILB	Detergent	Manchester International Freight Terminal
80 7998 002-9	ICB	Sodium	Deeside Titanium, Dee Marsh
80 2796 069-3	IPB	Wine	Warrington Dallam

Note 1: Rather than returning them abroad empty the two German IMBs had been redirected from Harwich to collect an export load of ball clay from the English China Clay works at Marsh Mills.

Note 2: The first three wagons were to be detached at Whitemoor where they would be attached to train 6V85, the Whitemoor–Severn Tunnel Junction Speedlink. Train 7M86 also called at Ipswich and Toton *en route* to Warrington, and non-ferry traffic would also be conveyed when available.

6M61 Dover–Willesden, 28 September 1987 (locomotive No 33 049)

Wagon number	Type	Load	Destination
70 7398 065-6	TIB	Bromine	Associated Octel, Amlwch
70 7490 357-0	TIB	Bromine	Associated Octel, Amlwch
80 2795 017-2	IPA	Chipboard	P. & G. Fogarty, Blackburn
70 7490 247-7	TIA	Anti-knock compound	Associated Octel, Ellesmere Port
70 7490 251-9	TIA	Anti-knock compound	Associated Octel, Ellesmere Port
71 2148 436-1	ITX	Fruit	Transfesa, Wavertree
71 2148 613-5	ITX	Fruit	Transfesa, Wavertree
70 2795 324-4	PIA	Chipboard	Brierley Hill
83 2797 088-1	ILA	Domestic appliances	Lansdown International, Didcot
83 2797 134-3	ILA	Domestic appliances	Lansdown International, Didcot
83 2797 166-5	ILA	Domestic appliances	Lansdown International, Didcot
70 7277 365-6	TIX	Anhydrous dimethylamine	ICI, Haverton Hill
83 2382 200-5	ILB	Groupage traffic	Railstore, Gidea Park
71 2396 038-4	ITX	Fruit	Sheffield Parkway Market
83 8089 232-3	IIB	Fruit	Sheffield Parkway Market
83 8089 931-0	IIB	Fruit	Minilink, Willesden
83 8089 751-2	IIB	Fruit	Luton
87 5699 016-8	IPB	Silicate sand	Dow Corning, Barry Docks
B 954537	CAR		Willesden Yard

Note 1: All five tank wagons had in fact returned to Britain for reloading but are shown loaded as they would still contain traces of their previous load and as such were treated as dangerous. On TOPS they would appear as Category D (discharged), Category E (empty) being applicable to such tanks only when they had been purged and therefore presented no potential hazard.

Note 2: The three Italian bogie vans, still coded ILA and with their original numbers, were carrying Ariston washing machines.

Note 3: Groupage traffic referred to a number of smaller items which, if travelling to the same destination, could be loaded in the same van. They were often items for mail order companies but in this instance the Italian van *en route* to Gidea Park was loaded with goods for the C&A chain of clothes stores.

Note 4: The inclusion of a brake van at the rear of an otherwise fully-fitted train for the guard to ride in was a requirement for all trains that included wagons labelled as containing toxic gases. In this case the Anhydrous Dimethylamine TIX returning to ICI's Haverton Hill works at Billingham.

A Class 33-hauled Dover–Willesden freight nears its destination in March 1980 with a typical mix of
ferry vehicles, including five Transfesa vans, two Interfrigo vans, an Italian van and a French van.
David Monk-Steel collection

6M86 Dover–Crewe, 6 May 1994 (locomotive No 47 312)

Wagon number	Type	Load	Destination
70 6094 046-7	ZDB	Buffers and wheelsets	Associated Octel, Ellesmere Port
83 2795 169-1	IMA		Mossend Euro-Transit, Mossend
83 2795 067-7	IMA		Mossend Euro-Transit, Mossend
80 2797 664-0	IWB	Chipboard	A. V. Dawson, Middlesbrough
80 2797 595-6	IWB	Chipboard	P. & G. Fogarty, Blackburn
70 4666 013-6	KIA	Cold-reduced coil	A. V. Dawson, Middlesbrough
70 9292 200-0	JIA	Cationic starch	Aberdeen Guild Street
70 9292 203-4	JIA	Cationic starch	Aberdeen Guild Street
80 7894 042-0	ICB	Ethyl chloride	Associated Octel, Ellesmere Port
80 7794 036-3	ICA	Ethyl chloride	Associated Octel, Ellesmere Port

Note: The two Italian bogie vans had come from Paddock Wood and were heading for Scotland to be reloaded with refractory bricks for the continent. Previously they had arrived in Britain with domestic appliances for the Whirlpool depot at Paddock Wood.

Nord Pas-de-Calais 18.30 sailing from Dunkerque to Dover, 6 January 1993

Wagon number	Type	Load	Destination
80 7996 007-0	ICA	Phosphorus	Albright & Wilson, Langley Green
80 7996 109-4	ICA	Phosphorus	Albright & Wilson, Langley Green
80 7996 006-2	ICA	Phosphorus	Albright & Wilson, Langley Green
80 4742 023-1	IGB	Long welded rail	Rotherham Masborough
80 4742 049-6	IGB	Long welded rail	Rotherham Masborough
80 4742 025-6	IGB	Long welded rail	Rotherham Masborough
80 4736 033-8	IGA	Long welded rail	Rotherham Masborough
80 4742 047-0	IGB	Long welded rail	Rotherham Masborough
80 4742 014-0	IGB	Long welded rail	Rotherham Masborough
83 2795 159-2	IMA	Glassware	Birmingham Landor Street
80 2793 014-4	IZA	Mineral water	London International Freight Terminal

Note 1: Long welded rail was among the more unexpected traffic to be seen on the train ferry, this consignment being for Balfour Beatty.

Note 2: The Italian IMA was loaded with car windscreens and windows.

Nord Pas-de-Calais 03.30 sailing from Dover to Dunkerque, 25 January 1993

Wagon number	Type	Load	Origin
87 7996 000-8	ICA	Toluene diisocyanate	Pan Ocean Storage, Ellesmere Port (Eastham)
87 7996 002-4	ICA	Toluene diisocyanate	Pan Ocean Storage, Ellesmere Port (Eastham)
80 2693 011-9	IWA	Rod coil	Scunthorpe Rod Mill
70 2795 302-0	KVA	Rod coil	Scunthorpe Rod Mill
70 2795 327-7	KVA	Rod coil	Scunthorpe Rod Mill
83 2795 065-1	IMA	Refractory bricks	Mossend Euro-Transit, Mossend
87 2380 681-4	ILX		Alsthom, Washwood Heath
80 2797 138-5	IWB	Bagged china clay	English China Clays, Drinnick Mill
80 2797 158-3	IWB		Railstore, Gidea Park
80 7895 011-4	ICB	Ethylene dibromide	Associated Octel, Amlwch
70 7490 284-0	TIA	Anti-knock compound	Associated Octel, Ellesmere Port

Note: Both French bogie ICAs were returning to the Continent discharged having delivered toluene diisocyanate to Pan Ocean at Eastham.

WAGON NUMBERING

From 1964 wagons that crossed international frontiers were given 12-digit numbers under a scheme devised by the International Union of Railways. Digits 1 and 2 were the exchange code and indicated whether a vehicle had bogies or fixed axles, if its gauge was variable or fixed, and the international body under whose jurisdiction it fell, although some types, initially worked by special agreement, would eventually become a standard design at which point their exchange code would be changed.

Exchange Codes applicable January 1990

01	Common-user non-bogie fixed-gauge railway-owned wagons in the Europ, OPW or Interfrigo pools
03	Common-user non-bogie fixed-gauge privately owned wagons in the Interfrigo pool
04	Common-user non-bogie variable-gauge privately owned wagons in the Interfrigo pool
06	Common-user non-bogie variable-gauge leased privately owned wagons in the Interfrigo pool
21	Non-common-user non-bogie fixed-gauge railway-owned wagons to RIV or PPW standard designs
23	Non-common-user non-bogie fixed-gauge privately owned wagons to RIV or PPW standard designs
24	Non-common-user non-bogie variable-gauge privately owned wagons to RIV or PPW standard designs
31	Non-common-user bogie fixed-gauge railway-owned wagons to RIV or PPW standard designs
33	Non-common-user bogie fixed-gauge privately owned wagons to RIV or PPW standard designs
34	Non-common-user bogie variable-gauge privately owned wagons to RIV or PPW standard designs
43	Two-axle privately owned wagons not to RIV or PPW standard designs, worked internationally by special agreement
83	Bogie privately owned wagons not to RIV or PPW standard designs, worked internationally by special agreement

Europ Pool	Western European railways wagons
Interfrigo	European railways refrigerated vans
OPW	Eastern European railways wagons
RIV	Reglomento Internazionale Vagoni (international wagon-standardisation regulations)
PPW	Prawila Polsowanij Wagonami (international wagon-standardisation regulations)

Digits 3 and 4 indicated the owning or registering railway, those of relevance to Anglo-Continental traffic being:

44	Budapesti Helyi Érdekű Vasút (BHEV) — Budapest Suburban Railway
54	Československé Státní Dráhy (CSD) — Czechoslovak State Railways
55	Magyar Államvasutak (MAV) — Hungarian State Railways
68	Ahaus Alstätter Eisenbahn (AAE)
70	British Rail (BR)
71	Rede Nacionale de los Ferrocarriles Españoles (RENFE) — Spanish National Railways
72	Zajednica Jugoslovenskih Železnica (JZ) — Yugoslav Federal Railways
74	Statens Järnvägar (SJ) — Swedish State Railways
80	Deutsche Bundesbahn (DB) — German Federal Railway
81	Österreichische Bundesbahnen (OBB) — Austrian Federal Railways
83	Ente Ferrovie dello Stato (FS) — Italian State Railways
85	Schweizerische Bundesbahnen (SBB) — Swiss Federal Railways
87	Société Nationale des Chemins de Fer Français (SNCF) — French National Railways
88	Société Nationale des Chemins de Fer Belges (SNCB) — Belgian National Railways

Digits 5-8 provided information on the operating characteristics of the wagon being determined from a set of guidelines that ran to more than 40 pages. These characteristics were also categorised by a sequence of letters found on the vehicles. Digits 9-11 gave the individual wagon identification while 12 was the check digit. This was included to allow the various railway computer systems to verify that there had been no error in recording the other 11 digits. Counting from the left, after multiplying all the digits in the odd positions (1st, 3rd, 5th, 7th, 9th, 11th) by two, while taking those in the even positions at their actual value, then the sum obtained by adding up all the resultant digits would always end in zero. For example, for the BR ferry van photographed at Barry (21 70 2380 251-5) the calculation would be: 4+1+1+4+0+4+3+1+6+0+4+5+2+5=40. Note also that the initials of the relevant international body (in this case the RIV) and the owning or registering railway (BR in this instance) were also included alongside the number.

Those ferry wagons built to conform to the British loading-gauge, which was more restricted than the so-called 'Berne gauge' used on the Continent, and suitable for transport on the train ferry were marked with an anchor symbol. Each type was allocated a page in the British Railways 'E' Diagram Book of Ferry Vehicles which listed the owner, number range, brake type, tare weight, capacity and overall dimensions. From 1994 vehicles suitable for operation via the Channel Tunnel also received a tunnel symbol.

The three-character TOPS code allocated by BR to the vehicle was also shown on the diagram, all international wagons registered to run on BR having codes beginning with the letters I (for wagons registered by foreign railway administrations) or F, J, K, O, P, T or V (for those registered by BR) while the third letter of the code indicated the wagon's brake type. Before 1991 fewer codes had been used for ferry stock so that all foreign-registered tank wagons were listed as IC, and privately owned vans and hoppers as IP.

TOPS type codes

FI	Two-axle Carfit
IB	Two-axle tank
IC	Bogie tank
ID	Special well
IE	Container-carrier
IF	Flat, open low
IG	Flat
IH	Coil carrier
II	Refrigerated van
IL	Large van
IM	Medium van
IO	Open high
IP	Double-deck car-carrier
IQ	Flask-carrier
IR	Bogie covered hopper
IS	Two-axle covered hopper
IT	Transfesa medium van
IU	Bogie curtain-sided van
IV	Two-axle large van
IW	Bogie large van
IY	Two-axle curtain-sided van
IZ	Twin van
JI	Bogie covered hopper
JR	Bogie open
KG	Two-axle container-carrier
KI	Coil-carrier
KK	Twin silo
KL	Open high
KO	Bogie swing-bed intermodal
KP	Bogie hopper
KV	Bogie large van
OI	Two-axle ferry tube
OJ	Two-axle ferry high
PI	Articulated car-carrier
TI	Two-axle or bogie tank
VI	Two-axle Ferry van / motor-car van
WI	Enclosed car-carrier

Brake codes

A	Air brake
B	Air brake and vacuum through pipe
Q	Unfitted, air through pipe
R	Unfitted, vacuum and air through pipes
X	Air and vacuum brake (dual-braked)

One of the most enjoyable aspects of a hobby is the friendships one makes with like-minded enthusiasts and this book is dedicated to the memory of Colin Wright, with whom I spent many happy hours searching out the more elusive members of the wagon fleet. I would also like to thank Trevor Mann, David Monk-Steel, Mark Saunders and Hywel Thomas, not only for permission to include some of their photographs in this book, but for the enjoyment of their company on many a 'wagoning' jaunt. Thanks must also go to the officers and staff of the Manchester Ship Canal Co for providing me with a photographic permit and taking the time to answer my many questions regarding their railway operations at Ellesmere Port. Finally, I must acknowledge the many railway staff who allowed access for photography into yards and sidings up and down the country since without their hospitality this study would not have been possible.

David Ratcliffe
Swinton
July 2009

Right: Every so often a mistake was made, and a wagon would come off the train ferry at Dover or Harwich that had no business to be there. When that happened it would be held at the port, and if possible its contents trans-shipped to another vehicle for forwarding. Meanwhile the miscreant, after spending a day or two on British soil while the paperwork was sorted out, would be sent back. An out-of-gauge Italian anti-knock tank, 21 83 0719 059-3, is seen at Harwich waiting to be returned to Zeebrugge in August 1979. *courtesy Trevor Mann*

RAILWAY-OWNED

Above and below: Given that so much of the rail traffic between Britain and the Continent comprised foodstuffs and manufactured goods it was not surprising that vans made up half of the overall ferry-wagon fleet and until the 1980s the majority were long-wheelbase two-axle vehicles with planked or plywood bodies and large sliding doors. Familiar to modellers by virtue of the long-standing Hornby model were the 40-ton British Rail ferry vans, of which 400 were built by Pressed Steel and Ashford Works between 1962 and 1964. At 41ft 11in over headstocks, with a 26ft 3in wheelbase, a 13ft sliding door and four sliding shutter ventilators each side

their design was much influenced by Continental practice. Originally numbered GB 786873-787022 and 787098-787347, they were soon given 12-digit numbers and allocated to diagram E.256. Coded VIX, they carried a multitude of commodities, such as tin cans from the Metal Box factory at Worcester, whisky from Johnnie Walker at Kilmarnock, Hotpoint washing machines from Grantham and Kelloggs cereals from Trafford Park, to name but four, before being phased out of ferry traffic in 1982. Subsequently a few VIXs were retained at Dunkerque and Zeebrugge for transhipment traffic, but the rest spent their remaining years working as barrier wagons or in engineers' traffic. No 21 70 2140 220-1 was about to be loaded with animal feed for Denmark when spotted at Alloa in August 1981, whilst two months later 21 70 2380 251-5 (ex 21 70 2140 251-6) was seen at Barry Coal Yard, carrying tyres from Germany. *Trevor Mann; Hywel Thomas*

Left: The BR fleet also included thirty 14-ton Ferry CCTs, built at Lancing Works in 1958, which were fitted with end doors for the export of expensive motor cars. By 1983 they had also been withdrawn from ferry use and when photographed at Ellesmere Port in June 1985 B 889016 (ex 21 70 2199 016-3) had been re-coded RBX and lettered 'BARRIER'. Note that at some point this wagon had been fitted with UIC roller bearings in place of its original UIC plain bearings.

Right: French vans were a common sight, although from 1981 only the 500 built by Frangeco in 1965 (E.304) crossed the Channel. They were of similar size to the VIXs but had 8ft 2in (2.5m) door openings, and their upper sides were a mixture of ventilators and steel sheet. Like the BR vans they went virtually everywhere (the author's records include over 130 destinations in Britain), imported wine and fruit being common loads. Other loadings of note included chalk, carpets, fertiliser, glassware, perfumery, television sets and various obscure chemicals.
ILX 21 87 2380 740-8 was carrying drums of acetyl chloride for the Ciba Geigy works at Grimsby when recorded in Immingham Yard in March 1991.

Left: Even more numerous were the 800 40-tonne vans owned by Ferrovie dello Stato. All these Italian vans had an 8m wheelbase, the first 300 (E.651) being of planked construction with four sliding ventilators each side and two small ventilators in each end. Built by Officine Mechanica del Stango in 1966, ILB 21 83 2382 237-7 (ex 21 83 2148 237, originally diagram E.329) is seen at Ardwick West in March 1987. Having arrived with bags of lemons, it was waiting to be reloaded with plastic goods for Modena.

Left and below left: The rest of the fleet had sheeted sides plus an extra pair of ventilators. Fifty were fitted with a brake cabin at one end while a further 50 had end doors. Domestic appliances, furniture and shoes were all regular traffic from Italy whilst in the months before Christmas and Easter wine and citrus fruits were handled in considerable tonnages. ILB 21 83 2382 338-3 (E.652, ex 21 83 2147 338-9 to diagram E.345), one of 400 Italian vans built by Officine Flore in 1969/70 is seen at Dover in April 1995, whilst 21 83 2382 636-0, another to diagram E.652, is unloaded at Blackburn after arriving with cases of wine for Waitrose in December 1997.

Below: Built in 1973, end-door van 21 83 2388 031-8 (E.653, ex 21 83 2147 031-0, originally diagram E.346) was spotted in June 1985 at Warrington C&W sidings, awaiting attention from the wagon fitters. Having arrived in Britain with washing machines for Paddock Wood, it had been stopped at Warrington with dragging brakes while *en route* to Glasgow International Freight Terminal to collect a backload of whisky. Such empty moves within Britain were common as the railway strove to reduce the imbalance in ferry traffic and increase the level of exports carried by rail.

INTERNATIONAL TRAIN-FERRY WAGONS

Left: Ferry vans from Eastern and Central Europe also visited the UK, most common being the 65 40-tonne Yugoslavian Railways vans built by Franco-Belge in 1971. Again similar in size to BR ferry vans, these 26-tonne-capacity vehicles could be spotted in many parts of the country. Imported furniture was an important lading for the type, but when photographed at Ardwick West in September 1986 ILB 21 72 2390 036-6 (E.415) had just arrived with boxes of dyestuffs for the cotton mills in Nelson and Colne. Once or twice a year one of these vans would also turn up at Ardwick loaded to the roof with hundreds of 'Moses Baskets' from Zagreb for a local wholesaler.

Right: Yugoslavian Railways also owned a batch of 100 small 36-tonne planked vans (E.199) built by Fabrika Wagona Krasevo. They measured 9.34m over headstocks and had a 5.7m wheelbase and a 2m door. Backloads for Yugoslavian vans included bagged china clay from the West Country and textiles from Yorkshire, while the small vans would occasionally carry drums of anti-knock compound from the Associated Octel plant at Ellesmere Port back to oil refineries in the Balkans. IMX 21 72 2191 075-5 waits to head south from Warrington Arpley on one such working in April 1987.

Left: Of similar design to the large Yugoslavian vans were 100 ILBs built by Czechoslovakian Railways in the late 1960s.
No 21 54 2140 605-3 (E.353), loaded with bags of powdered basalt for use in the manufacture of refractory bricks, was photographed at Blackburn *en route* to the Cast Basalt works at Rose Grove, near Burnley, in June 1979. The Burnley area saw more than its fair share of Czech vans, for in one of those strange quirks the NCL depot adjacent to Burnley Central station was another destination for the type carrying goods for F. W. Woolworth. *Trevor Mann*

Right: Slightly shorter, at 11.78m over headstocks, were the Austrian Federal Railways 32-tonne vans built by Hauptwerkgatte in 1956. With a 7m wheelbase, they had end doors and two 2m sliding doors each side. Sixteen permanently-coupled pairs, purchased by the haulage company Delacher & Co, handled groupage traffic between Vienna and the international freight terminals at Manchester and Stratford. Previously numbered in the 21 81 2141 xxx series, each pair was recoded IPB and received a single new number. IPB 43 81 2690 100-0 was recorded eight years after its ferry use ended at the Peak Railway Preservation Society site at Buxton in October 1991.

Left: In 1961 a batch of 150 39-tonne planked ferry vans (E.006) were built by Gebrüder Crede for the German Federal Railway. Fitted with four sliding ventilators each side, they measured 11.26m over headstocks and had a 6.8m wheelbase, their double sliding doors providing an opening of 3.975m; dual-braked, they could carry 27 tonnes. No 21 80 2140 035-1 was one of two IMXs noted at St Blazey in August 1987. Like many of the ferry vans illustrated in this book, these vehicles often carried backloads of bagged china clay from the various dries in Devon and Cornwall.

Right: Between 1965 and 1967 Crede also built a batch of 100 German vans fitted with two-piece sliding roofs, end doors and two 2m sliding doors on each side. Although the vans were seen in general traffic, these special features meant they were particularly useful for certain flows such as the movement of uranium ore concentrate to the British Nuclear Fuels Springfield works at Salwick, near Preston, the ore being carried in very large sacks that could be craned through the wagon's open roof. Long crates were another such load, and in April 1986 IMX 21 80 5795 025-3 was noted at Warrington, heading back to Germany with several crates of military equipment from the US Army base at Burtonwood. Faulty door locks were a weakness of the type, and they would often appear with the side doors partially open.

Above: No 21 88 2380 022-0 (ex 21 88 2140 022-1) was one of 200 Belgian 40-tonne vans (E.423) built by Arbel Industries in 1973. Measuring 12.78m over headstocks and with an 8.5m wheelbase, these ILBs had an off-centre reinforcing cross on their 2.63m door and four ventilators each side. This example was photographed passing Warrington Bank Quay in September 1986 *en route* to Manchester International Freight Terminal with boxes of detergent powder.

Below: In addition to its fleet of conventional two-axle vans the Société Belgo-Anglaise des Ferry Boats also owned 50 flexible-roller-roof wagons (E.479). Built in 1977, they measured 12.78m over headstocks and had a 9m wheelbase, while the sides were formed by two large opening panels. There were no end doors, but one end housed the roof-operating mechanism. They were popular for carrying bulky ferrous and non-ferrous metal loads such as steel sheets and tubes, tinplate and zinc ingots. No 21 88 5799 043-4 passes through Stratford in August 1984.

INTERFRIGO AND TRANSFESA

Left: Loads requiring refrigeration or temperature-controlled conditions were carried in Interfrigo vans variously registered by the Belgian, Hungarian and Italian railways. The Hungarian vans were dual-braked, measured 10.5m over headstocks and had a 6.6m wheelbase. A metre of the interior was taken up by ice bunkers, limiting them to a 19-tonne payload, and in Britain they were used mainly to carry soft fruits from Italy and Central Europe to the Continental Freight Depot at Hither Green, Superior International at Offord & Buckden and the London International Freight Terminal (LIFT) at Stratford, where a couple in silver livery were awaiting unloading alongside the customs clearance bank in the late 1970s. Coded IIX, several batches were built by VEB Waggonbau Dessau, East Germany, in the 1960s, numbered in the 12 55 8097 xxx, 8098 xxx and 8099 xxx series (sunsequently tenumbered in the 01 55 8480 xxx and 8580 xxx series.
David Ratcliffe collection

Left: The larger (12.78m-long, 8m-wheelbase) Italian-registered Interfrigo vans operated more widely and could be spotted up and down the country. In addition to imports of fruit, which were also their main traffic, a more gruesome load was in frozen pigs' lungs from Denmark to the petfood factory at Melton Mowbray. Occasional export flows included cheese from Stranraer to Germany, venison from Inverness to Italy and seed potatoes from Aberdeen to Austria. One of 980 40-tonne IIBs built by Snia Viscosa, Italy, in 1972, 03 83 8089 438-6 is pictured at Warrington in April 1991. Fitted with 2.7m plug doors, the majority carried 25.6 tonnes.

Right: The Spanish firm Transfesa was one of the train ferries' main customers, shipping fruit and vegetables to Britain. The company operated its own distribution depots at Paddock Wood in Kent and at Wavertree in Liverpool, but its distinctive vans could be found the length and breadth of the network. They had interchangeable wheelsets to enable them to run on either the standard gauge or the 5ft 6in broad gauge found on the Iberian peninsula, exchange facilities being located at Cerbère and Hendaye on the Franco-Spanish border. Until 1983 its fleet comprised more than a thousand wooden vans, the majority (E.010 and E.011), built in Germany in the late 1950s, measuring 11.22m over headstocks, with a 6.7m wheelbase and eight ventilators each side. They regularly worked to Ardwick West, delivering oranges and onions, 24 71 0285 258-6 being recorded in February 1983.

Above: Also spotted at Ardwick in January 1986, 24 71 2148 407-2 was one of 90 ITXs (E.215) built by Westwaggen in 1959. It was fitted with an open brake platform, which increased its length to 11.72m.

Above right and right: In 1983 Transfesa introduced a new fleet of more than 400 vans built by Tafesa, Spain, and Waggon Union, Germany, to a new all-steel sliding-wall design which allowed access to the entire floor area from both sides and facilitated loading and unloading by fork-lift truck from ground level. They measured 13.96m over headstocks, had a 9m wheelbase, were fitted with four ventilators on each side and could carry a 26-tonne payload. No 24 71 2396 186-1 is pictured unloading at Ardwick in July 1985, while 24 71 2396 124-2, sporting a revised company logo, was recorded at Warrington in October 2000. Like other operators, Transfesa lived with a high percentage of its vans' returning to the Continent empty, but backloads included cereals, chemicals, china clay and soap powder.

CARGOWAGGON

This page: Two prototype sliding-wall 45-tonne vans were built for Cargowaggon by Duwag in 1982, and a production batch of 146 followed between 1983 and 1985. Similar in size to the Transfesa vans, they were all hired initially to Ford and Volkswagen. The Ford vans replaced elderly BR pallet vans in moving automotive components between its works at Bridgend, Dagenham, Halewood and Swansea, while the other 60 worked from Germany to the VW spares depot at Wolverton before going into general ferry traffic *c*1989. The prototypes had flush side panels, as demonstrated by 23 80 2493 000-6 at Dover in June 1994, while one of the early production batch, 43 80 2384 012-9, was recorded at Halewood in January 1989.

Opposite page: For a time some vans were painted in Audi and VW colours, but these later received the standard Cargowaggon livery. Nos 23 80 2384 109-7 and 23 80 2384 132-9 were photographed from a passing train at Bletchley in August 1987, while 23 80 2398 505-0 (ex 23 80 2384 092-5) was recorded at Dover, having just come off the ferry with washing machines for Trafford Park, in 1995, by which date all these E.514-diagram vans had been renumbered at least once and recoded from IPA to IVA.

Above: Recorded at Blackburn in July 1997, 23 80 2492 001-5 was one of two IVAs built by Duwag in 1986 to diagram E.663. With a payload increase from 27 to 30 tonnes, the design was subsequently developed by Duwag into the Twin-Van, in effect a pair of two-axle vans permanently coupled, which dispensed with conventional buffing gear at their inner ends, bringing down the tare to give a combined payload of 62.5 tonnes. The first 100 Twin-Vans TOPS-coded IZA, numbered 23 80 2794 000-099 (E.668), were delivered in 1986/7, two further batches, 23 80 2793 100-149 (E.710) and 23 80 2793 150-199 (E.753), arriving in 1989 and 1991 respectively. In 1992 the first batch was renumbered 23 80 2793 000-099, and by 1999 all 200 had become 23 80 2929 000-199.

Below and above right: In international traffic the Twin-Vans carried a variety of commodities, such as chipboard, detergents, pottery, refrigerators, televisions and whisky, and they were also seen on several domestic freight flows, including beer from Park Royal, newsprint from Immingham, petfood from Shieldhall and cider from Taunton. Mineral water from France was another important traffic for these IZAs, and at least three were painted in Perrier livery, although they were soon to be found in general service, 23 80 2794 005-1 being recorded at Blackburn in June 1988 with a load of waste paper for Germany. Seen at Immingham in August 1999, 23 80 2929 064-6 illustrates the standard livery applied to these vehicles.

Above: In 1999/2000 GE Rail purchased from Waggon Union 100 Twin-Vans, numbered 23 80 2929 200-299. Built in the Czech Republic, they had a more rounded profile than previous IZAs, which increased cubic capacity and payload to 63-tonnes. Initially they were expected to carry automotive components between Germany and a BMW engine plant at Hams Hall, but when this traffic failed to materialise some were hired by VW to supply its new distribution depot at Birch Coppice, whilst others were leased to StoraEnso and UPM to carry paper and newsprint. Allocated diagram E.869, 23 80 2929 275-8 stands in Warrington Arpley yard in May 2002.

2. BOGIE FERRY VANS

Right: Bogie vans had never been common in Britain because so much of the Victorian infrastructure at goods depots and private sidings was inaccessible to larger vehicles. However, this changed in 1977 when German wagon-leasing companies Cargowaggon and VTG (Vereinigte Tanklager & Transportmittel) both introduced 80-tonne-glw bogie ferry vans for service between the Continent and Britain. For their day they were real monsters, the VTG vans (E.471) being 62ft (18.9m) in length, while the Cargowaggon vans (E.476) were even longer, at 71ft 5in (21.7m). Their sides consisted of three sliding doors, and they carried 55 tonnes, load-securing being facilitated by steel eyelets built into the floor. Cargowaggon 33 80 2797 546-9, spotted in the Ministry of Defence sidings at Bicester in September 1992, was one of 80 IPBs built in 1977 by Waggonfabrik. From 1997 these vans began appearing with the ends and solebar repainted blue.

Right: Built for VTG by Link Hoffmann Busch (LHB), IPB 33 80 2796 098-2 had recently arrived at Warrington Dallam with cases of wine when photographed in April 1986.

Below: VTG owned 140 of these Type F1 vans, which, like the rest of its fleet, worked to almost every corner of the BR network. In 1996 several were fitted with curtain sides and saw use in zinc-ingot traffic to Bloxwich, but they were not a great success, and by September 1997 33 80 2796 055-2 was in store at Longport.

Above right and right: Between 1978 and 1985 LHB built VTG a further 312 bogie ferry vans to a new sliding-wall design. The first batch of 212 (E.481), known by the company as Type F2, were 65ft 10in (20.06m) long and carried 53.5 tonnes, while the 100 Type F3 (E.593) were 73ft (22.22m) in length, uprated to 90 tonnes glw and carried 73.5 tonnes. Type F2 IPB 33 80 2797 133-6, seen at Stoke Wagon Works in June 1986, illustrates the original livery, while 33 80 2797 202-9 shows the revised scheme applied after sale to Tiphook; recorded at Ellesmere Port in April 1994, this wagon was carrying aluminium ingots from the smelter at Holyhead to Austria, one of numerous commodities that they handled over the years.

Above: Such was the popularity of the VTG vans that they were occasionally used on domestic freight workings within Britain, an example being the eight vans leased by Allied Steel & Wire to transport rod coil from Scunthorpe to Longport, Sheffield and Warrington, 33 80 2797 095-7 being seen at Scunthorpe on a very wet day in May 1987. After the opening of the Channel Tunnel all the Type F2 vans were leased by EWS for internal traffic flows.

Below: Unlike the F1 and F2 VTGs the Type F3 vans were not fitted with vacuum through pipes, these being no longer required after BR had dispensed with the last of its vacuum-braked wagonload services in 1984. Fifty of the F3s were registered in Germany and coded IPA (later changed to IWA), while the rest were registered by BR and coded PIA (later KVA). All remained in international service after 1994, and 33 80 2693 023-4 was photographed at Warrington in June 2001 loaded with paper towels, tissues and disposable nappies *en route* from Crailsheim in south-west Germany to the Creative Logistics terminal at Ordsall Lane in Manchester.

Above: Not to be outdone, Cargowaggon introduced its own two-door sliding-wall bogie vans in 1979. The main batch comprised 120 IPBs (E.512) built by Waggonfabrik, a further 50 IPAs (E.551) following from Waggon Union in 1983; all were 71ft 5in (21.7m) long and carried 53 tonnes. They saw use on various cross-Channel traffic, and a few were hired for workings within Britain. Still in its original livery when photographed in August 1991, 33 80 2797 660-8 had just arrived at Ordsall Lane with paper from the Continent.

Below: Two Cargowaggon vans, 83 80 2797 664-9 and 83 80 2797 687-9, the latter shown at Warrington in May 1987, were leased by Taunton Cider to carry bottled drinks from Norton Fitzwarren to the Isis Link depot at Law Junction, outside Motherwell, until ousted by Twin-Vans in 1989.

Left: Other Cargowaggon vans appeared with Perrier branding, while most colourful of all were the 16 vans repainted for bagged-cement traffic from the Blue Circle works at Hope. A freshly painted 33 80 2797 688-9 glistens in the sun at Warrington in July 1999.

Below left: Guinness also leased nine Cargowaggon vans to supplement the BR-owned vans used in beer traffic from its brewery at Park Royal to Liverpool. No 33 80 2798 007-1, from the 1983 batch, is seen at Spekeland Road in August 1989.

Above: Other bogie ferry vans included 30 built at BREL's Shildon Works in 1979 for Danzas (E.483). Similar to the three-door Cargowaggon vans but only 69ft 6in (21.1m) long, they carried 54 tonnes. For many years three were leased by ECC for bagged-clay traffic between Cornwall and the Potteries, but the others were in general ferry traffic, IPA 33 70 2797 005-8 being seen at Ardwick in July 1985 loaded with dyestuffs from Italy.

Left: Also registered by BR were the 15 sliding-wall vans built for Transfesa by Waggon Union in 1987. They were 72ft (22.14m) in length and carried 53 tonnes, but unlike the two-axle Transfesa vans these were not ventilated. Imports of mineral water and bagged fertiliser, along with exports of newsprint and whisky, constituted their principal traffic, but by 2004 all were working on the Continent. No 83 70 2795 350-9 was found in Trafford Park yard in April 1990.

Left: The 200 80-tonne bogie vans (E.553) built by Ferrosud in 1982 for Italian State Railways have always been regular visitors to the UK. Measuring 65ft 11in (20.06m) in length and capable of carrying 54 tonnes, they were fitted with Y25C bogies. They have handled a diverse range of commodities, car windscreens, domestic appliances and wine being common imports, while regular export traffic has included aluminium coil, china clay, tinplate and whisky. Originally numbered 31 83 2797 001-200 and coded ILA, they were re-coded IMA and renumbered in 1990 as 31 83 2795 001-200. No 31 83 2795 156-8 is seen at Middlesbrough Goods in March 2005.

Above: Among the most recognisable of all ferry wagons were the VTG coil vans. Measuring just 13.3m over headstocks, the first batch of 75, built in 1979 by LHB to diagram E.485, had five wells set into the floor to accommodate coils up to a total weight of 60.5 tonnes, while three telescopic sliding hoods gave access to any two-thirds of the vehicle either from the side or from above. Steel sheet or plate could also be carried by covering the wells with integral drop-flaps, but such was the vans' popularity in coil traffic that this feature was deleted, with a concomitant increase in payload to 65 tonnes, when a second batch of 80 was delivered in 1985. Offering all-weather protection and easy loading/unloading, they were used to carry coils of delicate 'bright steel' (used by car makers and manufacturers of 'white goods') and could be seen employed on domestic flows as well as in international traffic. The P. & G. Fogarty depot at Bolton Road, Blackburn, was a regular destination, 33 70 5899 022-3 from the first batch being recorded there in June 1994. At that date it was one of 32 VTG coil vans working between British Steel's Lackenby Works and steel stockholders in Blackburn, Wakefield and Wolverhampton.

Left: Unlike the original batch, which had all been registered by BR, the second batch of coil vans, built to diagram E.585, were split 30/50 between British and German registration. Middlesbrough Goods was also an important destination for domestic and international coil traffic, 33 80 4667 034-9 being seen there in May 2004. All VTG coil vans were eventually repainted blue following purchase by Tiphook in 1994.

Above: Built in 1987 by Waggon Union for general ferry service, Cargowaggon's 160 90-tonne Hold-Alls (diagram E.690) featured a two-piece telescopic hood. To open, one section was lifted and slid over the other by means of a mechanical transmission operated by the large hand wheels situated at each end of the wagon. Measuring 19.52m over headstocks, they could carry 63.5 tonnes. Here a partially cleaned 83 80 4741 117-1 receives attention at the Marcroft outstation at Ellesmere Port in September 1994.

Below: Visits to Ditton Creosoting Works, near Widnes, seldom yielded anything other than BR open wagons, but in August 1996 several ferry vans, including 83 80 4741 135-3, were observed arriving loaded with sawn timber from France.

Left: Until 1993 fifty Hold-Alls were leased by Norsk Hydro for fertiliser traffic from Immingham. A rainy day in October 1989 saw staff at the Russell terminal in Gartcosh unloading 83 80 4741 023-1.

Below: Another unique design appeared in 1995, when the Rover Group purchased 100 90-tonne Hi-Cube bogie wagons from Transtech, a division of Finnish steel company Rautaruukii. Designed to carry bulky but relatively lightweight body parts from the former Pressed Steel works in Swindon to the car-assembly plant at Longbridge, they were 76ft long and had a maximum payload of 59.5 tonnes. The three-piece moulded cover could be slid by hand, giving access to either half of the vehicle, while the central floor section comprised two parts which could be lowered hydraulically into the well between the bogies, maximising the wagon's capacity. Allocated diagram E.835, KSA 83 70 4739 029-5 was photographed outside the Swindon works in July 1996.

3. CURTAIN-SIDED VANS AND HOODED FLATS

Right: An innovative design introduced by Transfesa was the 80-tonne curtain-sided bogie wagon (diagram E.545), of which 35 were built by Arbel Fauvet in 1983. Measuring 19.35m over headstocks, they were among the last ferry wagons to be built with a through vacuum pipe. Initially numbered 83 87 4739 000-034, they carried 58 tonnes and were used in general ferry traffic, steel tubes from Corby and tinplate coil from South Wales being their main export loads, while imports included French apples and bagged fertiliser. IPB 83 87 4739 029-5, loaded with apples for Sheffield Parkway Market, is seen at Tinsley Yard in July 1986.

Below: Twenty similar vehicles were built for Norsk Hydro by Inge Trans in 1986 (E.598). Only the end walls were fixed, the one-piece hood formed from plastic-coated fabric sheet could concertina into the middle few feet of the wagon for loading, and they carried 'Big Bags' of fertiliser from the Hydro factory at Immingham to distribution depots in Scotland, South Wales and the South of England. Unfortunately they lasted less than eight years in fertiliser traffic before conversion into flats. Recorded at Immingham in September 1990, IPA 83 87 4746 009-9 presents an interesting weathering challenge to modellers.

Right: Tiphook also purchased a fleet of 90-tonne curtain-siders (or 'hooded flats', as it called them), when it entered the wagon-leasing market in 1987. Built by Arbel Fauvet, the 100 PIAs had a payload of 65 tonnes and could be fitted with removable internal side-webbing sections, supported by intermediate aluminium posts, to handle bulky loads such as beer kegs and paper rolls. No 33 70 4746 133-6 (E.684) is shunted at Dover in April 1995.

Below right: In 1991 55 of the hooded flats were fitted with coil cradles and renumbered 33 70 4666 000-054. Re-coded KIA, they carried imported coil to steel stockholders in the Midlands and the North East, 33 70 4666 011-0 (E.750), recorded at Middlesbrough Goods in April 1995, being one of 10 leased to Reed & Sutcliffe for coil traffic from Boston Docks.

Below: Re-coded KHA, the other 45 hooded flats continued in general ferry service and were fitted with new curtain sides in 1997. In February 2000 KHA 33 70 4746 154-2 had arrived at Warrington Dallam with wheel blanks from the Continent. This was then a regular working, the wheel blanks being destined for finishing at the AdTranz works in Manchester. AdTranz occupied the old Taylor Bros site in Trafford Park which had lost its rail connection in 1983, but why these wagons could not have been unloaded on that part of the Trafford Park Estate rail system that remained in operation is a mystery.

Above right: One of 100 IHA (E.796) 57.5-tonne-capacity steel coil wagons, SNCF's 31 87 4667 069-0 was photographed at Blackburn in April 1994, soon after being built by Arbel Fauvet.

Right: Loaded with coil from Sollac's cold rolling mill at Biache St Vaast, near Arras, the IHAs quickly became a common sight in Britain, and a second batch of 100 (E.857) uprated to carry 68 tonnes was introduced in 1998. Both batches were also used to move specially coated coils from Shotton to Germany, and in 2003 EWS hired 60 to work from the steelworks at Llanwern and Port Talbot. At the same time wagons began appearing with a prominent yellow circle (painted on the hood), which, it is understood, was meant to identify a vehicle allocated to domestic coil movements, and not that it had been reassigned to banana traffic! IHA 33 87 4767 007-0, from the 1998 batch, waits to be unloaded at Middlesbrough Goods in June 2004.

4. COVERED HOPPERS AND POWDER WAGONS

This page: Covered hoppers became a significant part of the ferry wagon fleet in the 1970s, when several 80-tonne designs appeared. First on the scene, in 1974, were 65 British-registered Polybulks (E.431) built by Fauvet Girel and originally numbered 21 70 0999 000-064. They carried 57.3 tonnes and at 48ft 6in (14.8m) over headstocks were suitable for china clay and grain. Initially they worked in block trains of 11 wagons carrying feed grain from France to Pinhoe, near Exeter, but by the late 1970s the majority were in china-clay traffic from the West Country to Switzerland. Delivered in a two-tone livery with yellow lettering, they were gradually repainted an overall green, although this was a slow process. PIA 33 70 9382 032-8, renumbered but still wearing its original coat of paint, was recorded at Stoke Wagon Works in March 1990, while two variants of the Traffic Services livery are illustrated by 33 70 9382 026-0 and 33 70 9382 032-8, both also at Stoke, in June 1991.

Opposite page: By October 1983 only 40 Polybulks were listed on the original diagram, the other 25 having been sold to Ermewa, Nacco and Tiger Rail. Subsequently renumbered and reallocated to diagram E.644, some remained in china-clay traffic, among them 33 87 5699 011-9, by now owned by Ermewa and spotted at P. D. Stirling's Mossend terminal in March 1989, and 33 87 5699 019-2, recorded later that year at the Coalville Open Day.

Above: The Polybulks were used to transport calcified seaweed from Cornwall and granulated fertiliser from Immingham, while between 1982 and 1986 up to a dozen were allocated to Pool 0567 for patent fuel traffic between Hucklehoven and coal-concentration depots in the South of England and East Anglia. No 33 87 5699 012-7 is propelled into Western Fuel's Wapping Wharf depot in Bristol in August 1983. *Hywel Thomas*

Left: A longer-term working entailed the movement of silicate sand from the Pechiney Electro-Metallurgie works at St Julien in the Côte d'Armor region of France to Dow Corning at Barry Docks. IPB 33 87 5699 025-9 was so employed when photographed at Cardiff Tidal Sidings in August 1991.

Left: Also built by Fauvet Girel in 1974 were 66 Belgian-registered slab-sided Polybulks (E.442) that measured 17.04m over headstocks and were suitable for grain and plastics. With a maximum payload of 59 tonnes, they also carried imported poultry feed to Pinhoe, but by 1982 they were in domestic grain traffic, and when spotted at Ellesmere Port in April 1983 33 88 9380 040-3 was *en route* to Birkenhead with wheat from East Anglia.

Right: After purchase by CITA and renumbering the Belgium Polybulks became less common but still occasionally turned up loaded with malted barley from the Continent. IPB 33 88 9282 005-5 was *en route* from France to Carlisle when photographed at Warrington Walton Old Junction in July 1989.

Below: In 1990 three of the slab-sided Polybulks were renumbered again, having been acquired by Nacco to move imported urea from King's Lynn docks to the Ciba-Geigy plastics factory at Duxford. Repainted blue, 33 87 9384 001-2 had also gained 'Hydro' badges (Hydro's plant in the Netherlands being the source of the urea) by the time it turned up for repair at Standard Wagon, Heywood, in January 1992.

Right: Encouraged by the success of the first Polybulks, Traffic Services introduced a further 82 between 1981 and 1984. Built by Fauvet Girel, they were 2.25m longer than the earlier batch and were dedicated to grain traffic, which subsequently increased from less than 100,000 tonnes in 1981 to more than 800,000 by 1986. Grainflow PIA 33 70 9280 064-4 (E.561), loaded with 58 tonnes of wheat from Sandy for the Spillers Homepride mill at Birkenhead, was recorded at Ellesmere Port Yard in April 1986.

Left and below left: In 1983 another French company, CFMF, built 30 covered hoppers (E.538) for Scottish Malt Distillers Ltd. Similar in length to the Grainflow Polybulks, they were quite different in cross-section, with a flatter side. Used to transport barley from loading-points in East Anglia to maltings north of the border, they could occasionally be found carrying backloads of malt. In August 1984 a couple were photographed heading north through Peterborough in a Speedlink working, while in July 1988 PIA 33 70 9280 022-2 was recorded in the grain-unloading shed at Ordsall Lane, having arrived with a load of malt from Roseisle. Note that in the interim the wagons had been re-lettered.

Above: In 1984 thirty more covered hoppers (E.574) were built by Fauvet Girel for Storage & Transport Systems Ltd to handle imported grain derivatives such as rape seed and tapioca from a new trans-shipment point at New Holland, near Immingham. Unlike the Grainflow and Distillers Polybulks the STS wagons were also regularly seen in international traffic, carrying animal feed, malt and sugar. Almost-new PIA 33 70 9382 123-5 passes March in August 1984.

Left: When BR closed the Speedlink network the Grainflow and STS fleets were sent to work abroad, but in 1998 six former Grainflow Polybulks were repatriated by EWS for use on various trial flows. However, none of these developed into long-term contracts, and after some months in store at Longport the Polybulks returned to France. Renumbered, repainted and re-coded, IRB 33 87 9383 015-3 waits at Longport in February 1999.

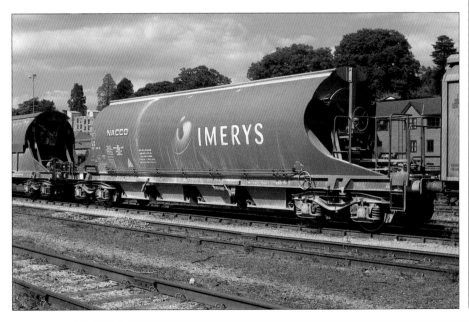

Left: In June 2000 the first Polybulks were finally replaced on the china-clay workings to Europe by 26 90-tonne-glw, 63-tonne-capacity bogie covhops (E.879) built for Nacco by Arbel Fauvet. Leased to Imerys, the successor to English China Clays, JIA 33 70 0894 008-8 was photographed in Exeter Riverside Yard some 12 months later.

Above: Between 2001 and 2003 Nacco also purchased a similar fleet of 53 bogie covhops from Arbel Fauvet for use by Cleveland Potash on potash and rock-salt workings from Boulby to Middlesbrough and Tees Dock. JIA 33 70 0894 122-7 awaits discharge at Middlesbrough Goods in March 2005. Note that the broad white stripe painted on the side features on only about a third of the fleet.

Left: Twenty-one 40-tonne STS twin-cone two-axle powder wagons were built by Ateliers de Joigny, France, in 1985 using second-hand underframes modified with parabolic springs. Twenty were leased by Tunnel Cement to work from the cement works at Tring and Clitheroe to Southampton, while the first vehicle, PIA 23 70 9192 002-3 (E.589) pictured at Marcroft Engineering, Coalville in July 1987, was used briefly in chalk traffic from France to Crewe.

Left: Among the many wagons built by Arbel Fauvet in 1987 for Tiphook were a batch of 15 90-tonne twin-compartment powder wagons (E.689). Fitted with Y25LS bogies, they measured 17.66m over headstocks and had a 65-tonne carrying capacity. Tiphook's publicity brochure listed more than 20 commodities for which they were suitable, ranging from alumina to talc, but they attracted little interest until 1991, when they were leased by Cerestar to transport cationic starch (starch with a positive charge) from Terneuzen to the paper mills around Aberdeen. They also ran to Cerestar's Trafford Park factory in Manchester, and in 1996 this became their base when they took over the domestic starch flows from the elderly fleet of Procor JBA and PCA wagons. JIA 33 70 9292 213-3 was heading back to the Netherlands when photographed in Trafford Park West Sidings in November 1991.

5. BOGIE HOPPER WAGONS

Left: Given the low value and widespread availability of most commodities carried in open hopper wagons there was little prospect of any international traffic. However, in 1988 Tiphook introduced a fleet of 150 ferry-fitted 90-tonne hoppers, presumably with a view to using them on short-term aggregate flows on either side of the Channel. In the event most remained in Britain, working for the various stone companies, until they were converted into Autoballaster vehicles in 1999. All were built by Arbel Fauvet and measured 15.33m over headstocks, but 83 70 6905 000-049 (E.700) had a slightly lower tare than 83 70 6905 100-199 (E.702). Embellished with a Brett logo but otherwise in original condition, 83 70 6905 103-0 is seen loaded with 67 tonnes of sea-dredged aggregate at Cliffe in May 1989.

Right and below: In 1990 Arbel Fauvet also built 24 90-tonne hoppers for Tiger Rail, to be used by ECC Quarries on the granite traffic from Croft to Bow and Bishops Stortford. In 1993 they were purchased by Nacco and later repainted, first in Camas livery and then in Bardon colours when the quarry changed hands. PIA 33 70 6905 068-6 is pictured at Stoke in April 1993, while 33 70 6905 073-6, the last of the fleet, was recorded at Croft in August 1997.

6. HIGHS AND LOWS

Left: In 1957/8 BR's Lancing Works built 40 21-ton high goods wagons (B 715000-39) for Continental service. Allocated diagram E.125 and UIC numbers 21 70 6190 000-039, they measured 23ft over headstocks and had a 14ft 10in wheelbase, with cupboard doors above a 5ft drop side door. Dual-braked, they had Continental-style oil axleboxes and buffers and chaining-down lugs along the solebar. Initially coded OIX after withdrawal from ferry service in the 1970s they became OJXs, and most ended their days on engineering duties. ADB 715027 was one of two former ferry highs re-coded ZGA used to carry railway equipment for the CMEE, Southern Region. Repainted from its original bauxite in 1987, it looked rather worn at Newport in March 1995.

Below: In 1959 Darlington Works built 20 dual-braked Tube wagons for BR, numbered B 733220-39. At 32ft over headstocks with an 18ft 6in wheelbase they were similar to standard Tubes but had on each side a pair of large drop doors separated by a removable stanchion. Additional fittings included a large document clip, triangular-based lamp irons, handrails and steps at opposite corners and chaining-down lugs. Although lettered 'TUBE' they were 26-tonne multi-purpose merchandise wagons and regularly transported large crates or small vehicles to and from the Continent on behalf of the military. Allocated diagram E.247 and numbered 21 70 6190 040-059, they later became 21 70 6094 040-059, and in 1982 the majority passed to the engineers, six being retained to work alongside foreign low-sided opens carrying wagons parts across the Channel. Previously coded OIX, recently repainted 21 70 6094 046-7 was still in ferry traffic when photographed at Ellesmere Port in May 1994, having just arrived from Dover with replacement buffers and wheelsets for a ferry tank wagon that had derailed inside the nearby Associated Octel plant.

Above right: French low 21 87 4145 244-5 was also loaded with wheelsets when encountered at Stoke Wagon Works in September 1996.

Below right: The shipment of new bogies was another significant traffic, and 21 87 4145 249-2 is pictured outside Standard Wagon, Heywood, loaded with Y25CS bogies in August 1989.

44

Left: Motor bogies for the Eurostar power cars being assembled by GEC-Alsthom at Washwood Heath were also handled, and 21 87 4145 265-8 was one of three sheeted IFBs waiting to enter the works on 23 April 1995.

Below left: Seen at Washwood Heath on 23 April 1995, 21 87 4145 206-2 was returning to France with a stack of the now empty cradles in which the Eurostar bogies had been delivered. All the French IFBs were from a fleet of 100, built for SNCF by Frangeco in 1967, measuring 12.62m over headstocks and with an 8m wheelbase. They could carry 28.5 tonnes and were allocated diagram E.342.

Above: In addition to railway equipment, other loads for the type included agricultural machinery and military vehicles, and as the ends and sides were removable they were often used as runner wagons under overhanging loads. No 21 87 4145 266-6 performs just such a role at Longport in October 1991, being marshalled between two bogie Cargowaggon flats that were loaded with long steel sections from British Steel's Shelton Works at nearby Etruria.

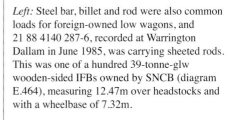

Left: Steel bar, billet and rod were also common loads for foreign-owned low wagons, and 21 88 4140 287-6, recorded at Warrington Dallam in June 1985, was carrying sheeted rods. This was one of a hundred 39-tonne-glw wooden-sided IFBs owned by SNCB (diagram E.464), measuring 12.47m over headstocks and with a wheelbase of 7.32m.

Left: Built by Link Hoffmann Busch in 1962/3, the 130 dual-braked German Federal Railway-owned 40-tonne-glw lows (E.259) numbered 21 80 4142 025-154 were known as 'stake wagons' on account of the shape of their removable stanchions. Capable of carrying 27.5 tonnes, they measured 11.26m over headstocks and had a 6.8m wheelbase. When photographed at Ellesmere Port in January 1987, 21 80 4142 113-0 was one of five two-axle lows newly arrived from Eastern Europe with a consignment of flasks and drums used by Associated Octel to carry anti-knock compound.

Left: Mineral wagons were relatively uncommon in ferry traffic, although SNCF provided fifty 40-tonne high-sided opens fitted with two pairs of full-height cupboard doors each side, and the Société Belgo-Anglaise des Ferry Boats owned twenty 39-tonne opens built by Waggonfabrik Uerdingen in 1971 (E.377). The Belgian Highs measured 8.76m over headstocks, had a 6m wheelbase and featured centrally situated cupboard doors and top-hung opening ends. Carrying 27.5 tonnes, these IOBs handled some unusual commodities, ranging from animal hides and skins to ferrous and non-ferrous ores such as barites, while a regular export working saw them loaded with copper and lead dross from the Commonwealth Smelting works at Avonmouth. No 21 88 6094 002-0 stands in Margam Yard in April 1985. *Trevor Mann*

Below left: No 23 87 5756 432-6 was a 45-tonne-glw open purchased second-hand by Tiphook in 1986. Built by Ateliers de Joigny in 1957, the type was widely used in France and the Low Countries but had not been seen in ferry traffic. However, after purchase this example was sent to Standard Wagon for modification which involved fitting BR parabolic springs and removal of the raised end sections. According to the ever-friendly staff at Heywood the intention was to modify up to 50 such vehicles, but after brief trials in scrap-metal traffic the idea was abandoned. Subsequently the wagon was renumbered 43 70 6094 432-3, recoded from IPA to KLA and sold to E. G. Steele, which used it to transport wheelsets from the Continent to its works at Hamilton. Allocated diagram E.671, it measured 8.76m over headstocks, had a 5.4m wheelbase and could carry a maximum payload of 29 tonnes. It is seen prior to modification at Heywood in September 1986.

Above: Towards the end of 1988 Tiphook began taking delivery of one hundred 90-tonne bogie opens from Arbel Fauvet (E.703). These measured 13.22m over headstocks and could carry 68 tonnes. A small door towards the right-hand end of the side was fitted for access and cleaning out, the vehicles being intended for spot hires. Initially they were employed by Foster Yeoman in aggregate traffic from Grain, and in subsequent years they have also carried stone on behalf of ARC, Bardon and RMC. All were domestic flows, but in 1991 three of these JRAs took over the copper-dross working from Avonmouth, and to avoid the time-consuming task of sheeting the wagons before each journey they were fitted with hinged covers. No 33 70 6790 026-2 had just been so modified at Stoke in February 1991.

Below: Other short-term traffic for the JRAs included agricultural lime from Thrislington to Inverurie, rock salt from Boulby to Middlesbrough and steel scrap from Trafford Park to Cardiff. Seen at Trafford Park in October 1995, 33 70 6790 053-6 displays the smaller Tiphook logo, as applied to the second half of the fleet.

7. CARGOWAGGON FLATS

Left: At the same time as it was investing in new vans Cargowaggon also purchased a fleet of bogie flat wagons for ferry traffic. Four batches of 50 wagons apiece were built by Waggon Union, all measuring 20.46m over headstocks (apart from the last batch, which were noticeably longer, at 22.6m), with eight collapsible stanchions per side and removable end stanchions. The end boards could be folded down for loading/unloading at end platforms if required, but this facility was rarely needed, for although they occasionally carried agricultural machinery their main traffic comprised steel and timber products. A grubby IPB 33 80 4742 036-3 from the original 80-tonne-glw batch (E.502) built in 1979 is seen at Warrington Dallam in March 1989, loaded with scaffolding board from Luxembourg.

Above: From the second batch (E.557) delivered in 1983 the design was uprated to 90 tonnes glw, maximum payload increasing from 57 to 66 tonnes. Originally numbered 33 80 4747 000-049, the second batch became 33 80 4647 000-049 in 1989 and were subsequently recoded from IPA to IGA. No 33 80 4647 035-1 had a sheeted load of steel tubes for Longport when photographed at Washwood Heath in April 1995. This was a regular traffic to Longport, the tubes being taken thence by road to a customer near Derby.

Left: Like the first batch the second had 10 wooden bolsters, albeit spaced differently, but these were fixed, whereas those fitted to the first batch were hinged and could be folded down into appropriate floor recesses. An empty 33 80 4647 037-7, with only its nearside stanchions in the raised position, leaves Longport in September 1995.

Left: The third batch of Cargowaggon bogie flats (E.670) were built in 1986 as 33 80 4737 000-049. Subsequently renumbered 33 80 4736 000-049, they had low-profile turnover bolsters, seen in the lowered position as IGA 33 80 4736 025-4 passes Didcot with imported rod coil in July 1994.

Right: These wagons also carried export traffic, and 33 80 4736 045-2 was one of two flats observed loaded with square tubes at Tees Yard in February 1999.

Below: The tubes originated at BSC's 20in mill in Hartlepool, and after loading the wagons were tripped to Tees Yard to be sheeted before continuing their journey to Italy.
No 33 80 4736 020-5 waits to head south from Teesside on a sunny day in September 1999.

Above: The fourth batch, built in 1990 to diagram E.726 and numbered 83 80 4736 100-149, were frequently used to carry steel sections from BSC's Shelton Works, although even their extra length was insufficient to cope with very long beams without the aid of a runner wagon. IGA 83 80 4736 130-1 is pictured in Longport Pinnox Branch Sidings with a load of 80ft beams for Cologne in October 1991.

Left: Unfortunately the steel-section traffic to the Continent, which averaged five or six wagons a week, ended when Shelton Works closed in April 2000. Cargowaggon flats were also occasionally loaded with export timber at Longport, 83 80 4736 115-2 being recorded in March 1993 with tree trunks destined for a furniture company in Breteuil, near Amiens.

Left: Shown on the TOPS computer as 'Building Material, Other', 83 80 4736 129-3 was in fact loaded with fibre cement sheets (the modern replacement for asbestos cement roofing) when photographed at Carlisle London Road in July 1995. In transit the bundles of sheets, which came from Italy, were secured with polyester straps attached to the 10 fixed winches along each solebar, but these had been removed and the wagon's side stanchions lowered prior to unloading. Note also the temporary wooden end supports.

8. TIMBER CONVERSIONS

Above: In 1989, to cope with a shortage of wagons suitable for carrying short lengths of timber, six E.502 Cargowaggon bogie flats had canvas side sheets fitted between the stanchions. Leased by BR, they ran loaded from Keith, Huntly, Inverurie and Inverurie to the Caberboard factory at Irvine, but all had returned to ferry service by 1991. No 33 80 4742 020-7 was photographed in Mossend Yard in July 1990.

Below: In 1990 Cargowaggon also converted one of the former curtain-sided wagons (diagram E.545), which it had acquired in 1989, by replacing the hood with 18 stanchions along each side. Renumbered and re-coded IOB, 33 87 4737 015-7 remained a one-off. It is seen at Warrington in May 1998 while *en route* from Crianlarich to the Kronospan board mill at Chirk.

9. FERRY TANKS

Left: Numerous types of ferry tank wagon were built, often in small batches for particular chemical traffic. In the immediate postwar era production of chlorine-based compounds increased enormously, and in 1954 Pickering built 20 anchor-mounted 20-ton-capacity two-axle tanks for Imperial Chemical Industries. All had full ferry fittings, including Continental roller bearings and a handbrake platform at one end, which was standard practice on the Continent. No 21 70 0785 010-0 is pictured at Stoke after withdrawal in December 1985.

Right: The Pickering-built tanks measured 24ft over headstocks, had a 14ft 10in wheelbase and were used to carry solvents such as trichloroethylene or Cereclor (a chlorinated paraffin wax) from the ICI works at Runcorn and Burn Naze. Depending on the characteristics of the chemical to be transported, barrels of greater cubic capacity could be attached, and 21 70 0785 015-9 was fitted with a larger barrel, having last carried orthodichlorobenzene, when photographed out of use at Burn Naze in February 1987. On TOPS 21 70 0785 010.0 and 21 70 0785 015-9 were coded TIQ, being allocated diagrams E.161 and E.223 respectively.

Left: Also built by Pickering in 1954 were eight liquefied-gas tanks (E.162) for use between ICI's new fluorine plant at Runcorn and the Continent. They carried various chlorofluorocarbon refrigerants (CFCs), known by the trade name Arcton, the gases being carried under pressure, requiring a reinforced barrel that limited capacity to 16 tons. TIB 23 70 7392 002-5 was in store at Stoke by October 1989.

Above: In 1965 increased demand for CFCs, particularly in aerosol propellants, saw ICI lease eight 40-tonne air-braked two-axle Arcton tanks from VTG. Purpose-built by Graff Kommanditgesellschaft, they measured 8.26m over headstocks, had a wheelbase of 5.2m and carried 26.5 tonnes. As with many German tanks built in the 1960s the barrel was fixed high above the solebar. Three or four tanks of Arcton were despatched every month from Runcorn to destinations across Europe, and until the line's closure in 1981 they normally travelled to Harwich via Manchester Dewsnap and the Woodhead route. ICB 23 80 7394 005-4 waits to leave Runcorn for the Netherlands in August 1985.

Below: Concern over the impact of some CFCs on the ozone layer reduced demand, and the traffic ceased in 1989, but a limited flow of Arcton returned to rail in 2003. By that date not only had the two-axle tanks been scrapped, but the sidings into ICI's Rocksavage Works in Runcorn had been lifted, and consequently the bogie VTG tanks were loaded from a road tanker at Widnes Foundry Lane. Running on replacement Y25 bogies, 33 80 7894 023-0, recorded at Widnes in January 2006, was one of four 80-tonne tanks leased by ICI's successor, Ineos-Chlor. Built by Waggon Union in 1975/6, these came from a batch of 56 bogie tanks (E.467) which over the years were used on a variety of cross-Channel chemical traffic, including butadiene to Dow Chemicals at King's Lynn, methyl chloride to Dow Corning at Barry and ethyl chloride from Associated Octel at Ellesmere Port.

Above: In 1957 Charles Roberts, of Wakefield, built 46 35-ton ferry tanks for its wagon-leasing arm, Tank Rentals Ltd. Fitted with UIC double-link suspension, they measured 24ft over headstocks but had the more common 15ft wheelbase and carried 20.3 tons. Initially vacuum-braked but with a through air pipe, they were designed to carry Class B liquids (*i.e.* with a flashpoint between 73 and 141°F) and had heating coils so that viscous products could be discharged more easily. Their initial employment remains something of a mystery, but by the mid-1960s most (if not all) were working from ICI's Heavy Organic Chemicals plant at Billingham, being used to transport aromatic compounds such as cresol, which was widely used in the manufacture of disinfectants and pesticides. At least 11 tanks were air-braked and transferred from diagram E.120 to E.121, but all had been withdrawn by the time TIB 21 70 0780 338-0 was spotted on its way to the scrapyard at Stoke Cockshute sidings in August 1983. *Trevor Mann*

Left: ICI's Heavy Organic Chemicals division (later Petrochemicals Division) also hired from Tank Rentals several other batches of Charles Roberts-built ferry tanks. These included the 20 dual-braked 'Q' tanks introduced in 1964 to carry iso-octanol (a plasticiser alcohol) from Billingham and subsequently used to transport aqueous amines. Measuring 25ft over headstocks, all had a 15ft wheelbase and a gross laden weight of 40 tons, the first ten, 21 70 0780 399-408 (E.291), having a payload of 25.7 tons. In common with the rest of the Tank Rentals fleet all were acquired in 1976 by Tiger Railcar Leasing, and between 1989 and 1991 six tanks (399, 406/9/11/4/8) were modified to air brake only and sold to ICI, the others, including 23 70 7190 401-3, pictured at Stoke in December 1985, having already been in store for several years. When new this wagon had carried a BR-allocated number (501401), its Tank Rentals fleet number (A361) and, for good measure, an ICI fleet number (Q401).
Its first 12-digit UIC number had been 21 70 0780 401-6, and had it survived to be sold to ICI it would have become 23 70 7390 401-3.

Left: The rest of the 'Q' tanks, 21 70 0780 409-418 (E.391), carried only 24.5 tons and were renumbered 23 70 7286 409-418, while those purchased by ICI became 23 70 7490 409/11/4/8, 23 70 7490 414-3 being recorded at Crumps Wagon Works at Connah's Quay in September 1992.

Right: Tank Rentals also owned two batches of 40-ton liquefied-gas tanks built in 1962 and 1964, many of which were also leased to ICI. The 25 built in 1962 were used initially in propane and ethylene-oxide traffic and comprised second-hand stayed ammonia tank barrels fitted to new 25ft-long, 15ft-wheelbase underframes. Rebuilt with monobloc tank barrels in 1964, they carried 20 tons and were allocated diagram E.313. Initially numbered 21 70 0780 353-377, they were allocated revised UIC numbers in 1980, and renumbered 23 70 7277 357-3, seen awaiting repair at Stoke in June 1985, was one of six used to carry butadiene from ICI Wilton to Dow Chemicals at King's Lynn. This working ceased in 1987, after which their only use was in anhydrous-amines traffic from Billingham.

Left: Four vehicles were modified from dual to air brake in 1985 becoming 23 70 7492 367-370 and together with 23 70 7277 362/363/365/366 were sold to ICI. 23 70 7277 362-3, one of the TIXs, was recorded loaded with anhydrous dimethylamine at Warrington Arpley in October 1993. Note the sunshield on top of the barrel, a common Continental practice on liquid-gas tank wagons.

Left: Amines are derivatives of ammonia and were used widely as intermediates in the production of herbicides, insect repellants, pharmaceuticals and water-treatment chemicals, the rail tanks from Billingham supplying chemical plants in France, Germany and Switzerland. Indeed, such was the demand for anhydrous amines that ICI also leased 10 bogie tanks for this traffic from VTG and STS. The seven VTG tanks were drawn from wagons to diagrams E.467 and E.679, while the three STS tanks came from a batch of 12 (E.497) 80-tonne-glw, 46.4-tonne-capacity anhydrous-ammonia tanks built by Fauvet Girel in 1969 for hire to Albright & Wilson. Originally numbered 21 70 0798 012-023, they measured 17.05m over headstocks and had worked from both Thames Haven and Ince & Elton, transporting ammonia to the fertiliser works at Barton-on-Humber. Transferred to ICI in 1984, all remained in domestic ammonia traffic until 1991, when 33 70 7892 017/18/19 were added to the amines pool. TIA 33 70 7892 019-2 is pictured waiting to be tripped from Tees Yard to Billingham (Haverton Hill in railway parlance) in June 1994.

Left: IBB 23 80 7392 001-5, photographed from the steps of Belais Lane signalbox, Billingham, in May 1991, was one of six 40-tonne liquefied-gas tanks (E.594) built by Waggon Uerdingen, West Germany, in 1986. Owned by EVA (Eisenbahn Verkehrsmittel Aktiengesellschaft) and numbered 23 80 7395 400-405, they were all used to transport anhydrous amines from Billingham until 1991, when two were reallocated to aqueous amines, repainted and renumbered 23 80 7392 001 and 002. The aqueous-amines workings ended in 1993, but anhydrous-amines traffic lasted almost to the end of the train ferry, the last loaded tank sailing from Dover *en route* to the Ciba Geigy plant at Monthey, Switzerland, on 19 December 1995.

Left: In 1957/8 British Hydrocarbon Chemicals, a British Petroleum subsidiary, purchased six dual-braked 32-tonne two-axle tanks (E.113) to carry butadiene from its works at Grangemouth to British Geon's newly opened nitrile-rubber plant at Barry Docks. Built by Waggonfabrik Uerdingen, they measured 8.42m over headstocks, had a 4.5m wheelbase and carried a 17.2-tonne payload. Initially painted white with red banding (a livery then statutory for liquid-gas tanks), they were by 1980 in hexene traffic between Rotterdam and Grangemouth, but this working had just ceased when TIX 23 70 7392 400-1 (formerly 21 70 0785 400-3) was encountered at Stoke in July 1986.

Above: Other ferry tanks working to Grangemouth included seven 40-tonne Class A wagons (for liquids with a flashpoint below 73°F) which were used to bring in acetaldehyde for the production of esters and resins. Built by Charles Roberts in 1962 (E.253), they were also dual-braked, measured 25ft 1in over headstocks and had a 15ft wheelbase. No 23 70 7190 351-0 (previously 21 70 0780 351-3) is pictured at Stoke in June 1985.

Below: Also noted at Stoke in June 1985 were the three 40-ton solvent tanks built in 1965 by Charles Roberts to diagram E.311. At first they worked from the Distillers Company plant at Hull Saltend, but in later years they carried hexylene glycol (a wetting agent in lacquers and polishes) from Grangemouth. Pictured is 21 70 0780 419-8, the first of the trio.

Left: Acetaldehyde and Acetonitrile, a solvent used in the production of polypropylene film, perfumes and pharmaceuticals, were occasionally transported by rail between the Continent and the BP Chemicals works at Grangemouth and the ICI Organics plant at Maxwelltown, near Dumfries, in 80-tonne bogie tanks from a batch of seven (E.394), that measured 17.4m over headstocks, built by Fauvet Girel for Sotranpa in 1972.
ICB 33 87 7895 003-4 was *en route* to Creutzwald, near the Franco-German border, when spotted at Dover in May 1988.

Below left: Wagon hirers Algeco, CLMI and STS all owned fleets of ferry tanks. Between them Algeco and CLMI operated 200 vacuum-braked, 15ft-wheelbase, 40-ton Class A tanks built between 1963 and 1965 by Powell Duffryn, Metro-Cammell and Charles Roberts, to diagrams E.284, E.285 and E.286 respectively. Photographed at Cardiff Tidal Sidings in October 1981, TIW 21 70 0780 675-5 (E.285), one of more than 50 leased to Carless Capel & Leonard, carried petroleum distillates such as white spirit from its refinery at Harwich to both British and Continental destinations. *Hywel Thomas*

Bottom left: STS owned more than 60 air-braked 40-ton ferry tanks that handled a wide variety of chemicals, including benzene from Stanlow, cresylic acid from Four Ashes, phenol from Grangemouth and plastics intermediates from Ardwick. TIB 23 70 7190 206-6 (ex 21 70 0780 206-9), one of 20 built by Powell Duffryn in 1964 (E.288), is pictured at Warrington in September 1989. Note the through vacuum pipe and the steam-heating pipes just visible in the end of the barrel.

Above right and right: In 1978 five Algeco tanks (635/47/53/9/71) were air braked and modified to carry acetonitrile. This involved removal of the bottom outlet and the fitting of new discharge valves. Operated by Whyte Chemicals, they ran from Italy to Dewsbury Railway Street Goods and Immingham Dock tank farm. Dewsbury received one or two tanks a month, and 23 70 7390 671-9 (previously numbered 21 70 0780 671-4) is shown being unloaded at Railway Street goods yard in April 1986. To prevent the escape of any flammable vapour, nitrogen is pumped into the tank as the acetonitrile is transferred to the road tanker.

Above: Also dating from 1964 were 24 tanks built by Pressed Steel, allocated diagram E.339. At 26ft over headstocks they were 8in shorter than the Powell Duffryn batch but had the same 16ft 3in wheelbase. In the early 1990s four were in lithium-hydroxide traffic from Switzerland to Manchester International Freight Terminal. Now owned by CAIB, 23 70 7397 103-6 (ex 21 70 0785 103-3) had been tripped from MIFT to the Marcroft Engineering outstation at Trafford Park for repairs in September 1994.

Below: In 1965 the Sentinel works in Shrewsbury built, for STS, two dual-braked Class A ferry tanks with a 15ft wheelbase. Prior to appearing at Stoke Wagon Works in June 1992 TIX 23 70 7190 200-9 (E.296) had been carrying diethyl ether from Courtaulds Acetates, Spondon, to an explosives factory at Karlskoga, in southern Sweden.

Right: The next batch of 15 STS ferry tanks (E.341) were more specialised. Similar in size to the previous build from Pressed Steel, these were lagged and coiled, part of a fleet of 28 stainless-steel tank wagons hired by BP Chemicals in 1966 to carry acetic acid, formic acid and propionic acid from the former Distillers plant at Hull. Alongside the balance of the fleet, which were not ferry-fitted, they worked to Baglan Bay, Purfleet and Spondon as well as the Continent, but by the early 1980s 10 of these TIBs had gone abroad for good, and the other five had been leased by TSL for spot traffics. No 23 70 7397 126-7 (ex 21 70 0785 126-4) had recently been in acetone traffic from Immingham Dock to the Glaxo antibiotics factory at Ulverston when photographed at Stoke in September 1990.

Left: Cutbacks in the UK's production of inorganic chemicals in the early 1980s prompted BR and the wagon-hirers to try to promote rail's share of the spot market. Given the greater flexibility offered by road it was a tough nut to crack, but, with the Speedlink fast-freight network expanding, STS set up RailCALL, a subsidiary from which customers might hire a wagon for a single transit rather than take out a term-based lease, which was normal practice. The scheme proved a success and by 1985 had attracted over 50,000 tonnes of new chemicals traffic to rail. Five STS tanks built by CFMF in 1979 (diagram E.494) were amongst those available to RailCALL. Air-braked, they measured 7.85m over headstocks, had a 5.45m wheelbase and could carry a payload of 28.1 tonnes. In May 1985 four of the batch, 23 70 7390 027/028/029/031, were hired by Hickson & Welch to transport orthochloroaniline and orthotoluidene (dyestuffs intermediates) from Castleford to the Continent. Subsequently they were sent for cleaning and washing out at

Right: Subsequently the four TIAs were sent to Warrington Dallam for washing out and at least 23 70 7390 027-4, was hired by Laporte Chemicals to transport sulphuric acid to France. As Laporte's Baronet works, south of Warrington, had lost its rail connection in 1970 following the closure of the Manchester Ship Canal Railway's Acton Grange section, the traffic was loaded at Dallam, where there photograph was taken in June 1985.

10. ASSOCIATED OCTEL TANK WAGONS

Right: At its plants at Ellesmere Port and Plumley Associated Octel produced anti-knock compound (a mixture of tetraethyl lead and ethylene dibromide) for use in motor and aviation fuel and employed a fleet of specialised rail tanks to transport this highly poisonous chemical to oil refineries throughout Britain and Europe. Photographed at Ellesmere Port in April 1993, TIB 23 70 7490 283-2 (E.628) was one of more than fifty 40-ton anti-knock tanks built for Octel by Charles Roberts between 1961 and 1964. Originally dual braked, it measured 25ft over headstocks and had a 15ft wheelbase (the heavily insulated barrel being only 19ft long) and a capacity of 23.5 tons. All valves were situated on top of the tank beneath a lockable bonnet cover designed to protect them from damage in the event of an accident or fire. Tank wagons in anti-knock traffic were required to be painted either aluminium or dove grey with yellow side panels describing emergency procedures in four languages. The practice of painting the bonnet cover dark green was adopted in 1992, although the reason for this remains unclear.

Rght: Access to the Octel works at Ellesmere Port was via the lines of the Manchester Ship Canal Railway, and twice a day an MSC Sentinel 0-6-0 tripped wagons between the plant and BR's Ellesmere Port East Yard. Pictured in September 1991, MSC 3003 hauls a rake of tanks out of the Octel plant and across Oil Sites Road; it will then run round its train before hauling it up the steep grade to the BR yard. Immediately behind the Sentinel are two anti-knock tanks bound for Italy (via Dover), while the other wagons are a mix of loaded chlorine and discharged ethylene-dibromide tanks bound for Amlwch. Most unusually for Associated Octel, the first tank is in a filthy condition.

Left: Ironically, despite the move towards unleaded petrol, records from the MSC Railway reveal that, at least in the short term, rail traffic from Ellesmere Port to the Continent increased as Octel cut production at its European factories in favour of Ellesmere Port. In fact the number of anti-knock tank wagons despatched by Octel rose from 170 in 1989 to 394 in 1990, and to meet this upsurge 23 VTG two-axle anti-knock tanks (E.355), which until then had made only infrequent visits, were assigned to Ellesmere Port. Built by Graaff 1968, they were similar in size to Octel's own wagons but, with a lower tare, could carry 24.9 tonnes. IBB 23 80 7491 007-2 is pictured at Warrington in September 1990.

Right: Sodium and ethyl chloride, intermediates used in the manufacture of tetraethyl lead, were also transported by rail from Ellesmere Port to Octel's associated plants in France, Germany and Italy. Built by Standard Wagon at Heywood in 1985 and pictured at Ellesmere Port in January 1993, TIA 33 70 7996 002-3 was one of three 80-tonne Octel sodium tanks. Allocated diagram E.581, these were 15.95m long with 10m bogie centres but could carry only 45.7 tonnes of metallic sodium, as the internal pipework necessary to effect unloading brought the tare up to a whopping 34.3 tonnes. It may seem surprising that sodium should be transported in tank wagons, but its low melting-point of 97°C allowed it to be poured into the tank in a molten state and then heated up again upon arrival by pumping hot oil through a closed system of pipes inside the vehicle. Like all chemical tank wagons these vehicles were subject to a rigorous safety regime, spending considerable periods of time undergoing maintenance. As a consequence each of the three Octel sodium tanks made no more than six round-trips each year, running from Ellesmere Port to either the AK Chemie plant at Biebesheim in Hesse, northern Germany, or the Octel Kuhlmann works at Paimbœuf, on the Loire.

Right and below: When ethyl-chloride traffic from Ellesmere Port commenced in 1978 it was transported in two-axle liquefied-gas tanks leased from Tank Rentals, until VTG bogie tanks took over c1983/4. No 21 70 0780 394-8, the last of a batch of 20 TIXs built by Charles Roberts in 1964 (E.290), was photographed at W. H. Davis, Shirebrook, in November 1985, while ICB 33 80 7892 035-6 (E.467), complete with its original German bogies, is seen outside the Octel works at Ellesmere Port in January 1986. These tanks measured 17.66m over headstocks and carried 49.8 tonnes.

Above: Approximately 30 bogie tanks of ethyl chloride were sent to the Continent a year until in 1994 a fire closed the production plant at Ellesmere Port, and, in a complete reversal, Octel had to start importing this essential chemical from Germany. A new pool of 12 VTG bogie tanks was quickly established, comprising 10 to diagram E.467 and two 90-tonners (33 80 7794 035 and 036), part of a batch of six ICAs built by Link Hoffmann Busch in 1987 that were also seen in Britain in amines traffic from Billingham. Allocated diagram E.679, they were 18.41m long and carried 57.5 tonnes. Fitted with LHB82 bogies, 33 80 7794 035-5 glows in the afternoon sun at Ellesmere Port in April 1995, only a few weeks before the cessation of all rail traffic at the Associated Octel works.

Below: Octel also owned chemical plants at Hayle, in Cornwall, and Amlwch, on the Isle of Anglesey, where it extracted bromine from seawater. Most was used to produce ethylene dibromide, but any surplus would be sold to outside customers for use in pesticides and fungicides, and between 1960 and 1962 M. W. Grazebrook built three vacuum-braked 15ft-wheelbase tanks for bulk deliveries to Europe. As bromine is corrosive to steel the barrels, manhole flanges and covers were all lead-lined, the two manholes being to facilitate the clearance of bromine vapour for inspections of the lining while the wagon was in service. Given bromine's high density a small (15ft 8in-long, 4ft 7in-diameter) barrel was used, ensuring that the wagons centre of gravity came below the maximum permitted height. Pictured after withdrawal, saddle-mounted 35-tonne tank TIW 23 70 7192 294-0 (E.238) on the ground at Crumps Wagon Works, Connah's Quay, in March 1986.

Right : Crumps did a lot of work for Octel, and 43 70 7490 357-0 was photographed at Connah's Quay in September 1992. This was one of ten 40-tonne bromine tanks built for Octel by Charles Roberts between 1964 and 1970 (E.385). Air-braked, they measured 25ft over headstocks and had a 15ft 9in wheelbase. These tanks were transferred *c*1982 to Dow Chemicals but remained in ferry traffic, carrying bromine from Amlwch, until 1993.

Below: VTG bromine tank 23 70 7398 065-6 came from a batch of six built by Waggonfabrik in 1961 (E.445). Initially German-registered, it had a wheelbase of 4.5m and carried 25 tonnes. Of note are the handrail along the catwalk to the central filler and the spillage channel on the side of the tank. When spotted at Warrington in June 1986 it was heading back to Amlwch for another load.

Right: When Octel began to scale down its European operations in the mid-1980s it also began to export ethylene dibromide from Amlwch, using four 80-tonne bogie tanks hired from VTG. ICB 33 80 7895 011-4, built by Link Hoffmann Busch 1979 to diagram E.508, pauses in Ellesmere Port Yard before continuing its journey to France in April 1993. In addition to 33 80 7895 010-6 and 33 80 7895 012-2 (both E508) Octel also leased ICA 33 80 7996 000-5 (E.565), built by LHB in 1984, for this traffic.

11. OTHER FERRY TANKS AT ELLESMERE PORT

Right: Also to be seen at Ellesmere Port were wagons heading for the two tank farms owned by Pan Ocean Storage & Transport and GATX (formerly Unitank Storage), both situated two miles west of town, at the end of the Manchester Ship Canal Railway's Eastham branch. Pan Ocean opened in 1979 and began receiving deliveries of latex from Strasbourg, carried by a batch of sixteen 80-tonne Nacco Polysar tanks built for this traffic by CFMF; allocated diagram E.496, they measured 11.5m over headstocks and carried 58.3 tonnes. ICA 33 87 7992 015-0 was photographed at Ellesmere Port in May 1987.

Left: Occasionally latex also arrived in VTG or Etra bogie tanks. No 33 80 7995 006-3 was one of 10 general-purpose insulated 80-tonne ICBs built by Link Hoffmann Busch to diagram E.511 in 1979; measuring 16.66m over headstocks, they had a payload of 56.3 tonnes. Fitted with LHB77 bogies, this example is pictured standing in the loop outside Pan Ocean in March 1989.

Left: Spotted in Ellesmere Port Yard in April 1982 was 33 85 7995 504-2, a Swiss-registered ICB belonging to Etra SA of Zurich. From a batch of six built earlier that year in Switzerland by J. Meyer, it measured 15.7m over headstocks, carried 56 tonnes and had a 1.75° slope to the barrel. In 1982 Eastham had received 130 tanks of latex, but this requirement gradually dwindled to less than 30 by 1989 before ceasing completely in 1991. *Trevor Mann*

Right: Pan Ocean also received toluene diisocyanate and acetic anhydride from France, the former (used in the manufacture of polyurethane foams, elastomers and resins) arriving in 80-tonne bogie tanks leased by Rhone Poulenc from Simotra. Built by CFMF in 1979 to diagram E.510, with Y25CS2 bogies, the Simotra tanks measured 14.2m over headstocks. In June 1993 ICA 33 87 7996 004-0 was noted in Ellesmere Port yard waiting to be delivered to the Manchester Ship Canal Railway at Ellesmere Port West, from where an MSC locomotive would haul it along the Eastham branch to Pan Ocean.

Above: The Eastham branch was also home to a batch of 15 80-tonne tanks built by CFMF for Rhone Poulenc in 1981 to diagram E.522. Initially six tanks (33 87 7996 015/019/020/023/025/029) were allocated to the flow of acetic anhydride to Pan Ocean, while the other nine (33 87 7996 016/017/018/021/022/024/026/027/028) worked from the neighbouring GATX tank farm, carrying acetic acid to Courtaulds' fibre works at Spondon. On average three tanks a week were despatched to Spondon, and 33 87 7996 018/021/024 are seen leaving the GATX terminal at Eastham together with a Shell 45-tonne lubricating-oil tank behind MSC Sentinel 0-6-0 No 3004 in January 1991. The working to Spondon ended in 1993, but the acetic-anhydride traffic lasted until the end of the train ferry.

Above and below: Loaded with acetic anhydride from France, 33 87 7996 021-4 was photographed on No 11 siding at Ellesmere Port Yard in May 1994, while 33 87 7996 018-0, one of two that sported the large lettering, is seen at the same location in September 1990.

Above: In 1967 two 45-ton TIBs (E.343) were built by Charles Roberts for Tank Rentals. Initially leased to ICI for cyclohexane and later methanol traffic, they were long wagons, measuring 30ft 11in over headstocks and having a 19ft wheelbase. On approved routes in Britain they could carry 29 tons but for Continental and ferry-boat working they were limited to 23 tons 17cwt. Both were lagged and fitted with parabolic springs when leased to Shell Chemicals in 1986. Loaded with acetone *en route* from Stanlow to Glaxo at Ulverston, the second of the pair 43 70 7499 301-9, was photographed at Ellesmere Port in June 1992.

Below: CIE Auxiliare IB owned 10 Belgian-registered 40-tonne ICBs built in 1974 by SATI, Antwerp. Measuring 7.52m over headstocks, they had a 4.5m wheelbase, carried a 28-tonne payload and had been lagged when new. Loaded with lubricating oil, 23 88 7499 001-9 was photographed at Ellesmere Port while *en route* from the Continent to Birkenhead Docks in February 1982. *Trevor Mann*

Above: Until its closure in 1994 the Deeside Titanium smelter at Dee Marsh, near Shotton, received both sodium and titanium tetrachloride by rail. Two small batches of EVA bogie tanks carried sodium from a Degussa plant at Hurth, near Cologne, while a third batch owned by Métaux Spéciaux brought sodium from its works at Pomblière, near St Marcel in the Savoie *département* of France. Built by Waggon Union, all ten 80-tonne EVA sodium tanks measured 13.96m over headstocks and carried a payload of 48.5 tonnes. ICB 33 80 7998 002-9, built in 1980 (E.519), was recorded at Warrington Arpley C&W sidings in February 1987. The pipework on the side facilitated heating the contents prior to unloading, while the bars over the filler were to prevent accidental or unauthorised opening.

Below left: ICA 33 80 7998 903-8, one of the second batch of five EVA sodium tanks (E.548) built in 1982, is seen at Ellesmere Port in April 1994. By this date rail traffic to Deeside Titanium had ceased, and this wagon was in service with Associated Octel.

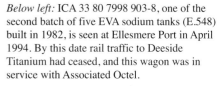

Above right: The six 80-tonne Métaux Spéciaux sodium tanks (E.546) built by Arbel Fauvet in 1982/3 were longer, measuring 15.25m over headstocks, and carried 50.9 tonnes. ICB 33 87 7996 041-2, the second of the batch, stands at Warrington Arpley in March 1986.

Right: Deeside Titanium reacted sodium with titanium tetrachloride to produce metallic titanium for the aerospace and automotive industries, five 80-tonne tanks, owned by Locatransport and leased to Thann & Mulhouse, delivering the titanium tetrachloride from a plant near Le Havre. Built by Arbel Fauvet in 1983, they measured 11.26m over headstocks and carried 60.2 tonnes. ICA 33 87 7896 016-5 is shunted at Dover in October 1989.

Above: The Dow Corning chemical plant at Barry, not to be confused with BP Chemicals or Dow Chemicals (both of which also had works nearby), underwent a £150 million expansion in the early 1980s to meet the worldwide demand for silicones and silicon compounds. In addition to the silicate-sand traffic delivered from France in Polybulks Dow Corning required methyl chloride, and this was transported by rail from Stade, near Hamburg, in five purpose-built 80-tonne VTG liquid-gas tanks (E.534) constructed by Waggon Union in 1982. First of the batch, ICB 33 80 7794 000-9 (previously numbered 33 80 7891 200-7) was recorded with faulty brakes on the repair track at Cardiff Tidal Sidings in August 1991. Relatively short vehicles, at 13.66m over headstocks, they carried 54.5 tonnes and were joined in 1987 by two similar tank wagons numbered 33 80 7794 015/016. Loading and unloading valves were located along the side at solebar level, the hatch on the end providing access just for cleaning and maintenance.

Below: In 1986 Dow Corning leased four new VTG 90-tonne Class A tanks (E.674) for methyltrichlorosilane traffic from Barry to Germany. Built by Link Hoffmann Busch with DBWU80 bogies, these ICAs measured 14.56m over headstocks and had a maximum payload of 64.4 tonnes. They were not easy wagons to photograph, the traffic being infrequent, but 33 80 7793 002-6 was spotted at Cardiff Tidal in July 1991. *Hywel Thomas*

Above: Following the closure of Severn Tunnel Junction Yard in 1987 Cardiff Tidal Sidings became the main centre for wagonload traffic in the area. TIA 33 70 7890 204-2, seen there in May 1992, was one of five 80-tonne hydrofluoric-acid tank wagons (E.715) built for CAIB in 1989 by Ateliers de Joigny. Running on Y25CS2 bogies, they measured 14m over headstocks, could carry a 56-tonne payload and, according to the pool header, were leased by the Imperial Smelting Corporation to work from Avonmouth to Yugoslavia. Hydrofluoric acid, produced at Avonmouth by reacting sulphuric acid with fluorspar, was used in small quantities for etching glass, but why the Yugoslavians in particular should have needed tankcars of the stuff remains something of a mystery. In any event the working ceased the following year. *Hywel Thomas*

Below: The last wagons to be built at Powell Duffryn Standard's Heywood works in 1992 were a fleet of 13 90-tonne vinyl-chloride-monomer tanks (E.783) supplied to Nacco. Unlike most ferry tanks, which tended to operate in ones and twos, they ran as a block train of nine to 12 wagons from ICI's Hillhouse Works at Burn Naze to the European Vinyls Corporation siding at Barry Docks. The valve gear for loading and unloading was located in the large chest beneath the solebar, only the pressure-relief valves being situated atop the tank barrel. TIA 33 70 7793 007-7 is reflected in the puddles on the quayside at Barry in October 1994.

14. FERRY TANKS ON TEESSIDE

Right: Several different 40-tonne two-axle VTG ferry tanks, all built by Graaff in the 1960s, were used to transport ethyl glycol from Dormagen, south of Düsseldorf, to Middlesbrough, including IBB 23 80 7391 006-5 (E.630), seen at Port Clarence in May 1993. This was a relatively long vehicle, measuring 11.16m over headstocks and with 7.8m wheelbase, whereas most tanks in glycol traffic were only 9.16m over headstocks, with a 6.7m wheelbase.

Left: Although the glycol was destined for the ICI works at Wilton the tanks were unloaded at Middlesbrough Goods, where IBB 23 80 7391 033-9 (E.372), one of the shorter vehicles, was recorded in September 1989.

Right: Another long-standing chemical traffic on Teesside was the movement of caustic soda on behalf of Atochem, ICI and Dow Chemicals from the tank farm at Seal Sands to customers in Cumbria and Scotland. Amongst the various tank wagons used over the years were two of the general-purpose bogie VTG tanks from diagram E.511. No 33 80 7995 009-7 waits to leave Tees Yard for the Roche Vitamin C factory at Dalry in September 1997.

Right: Five 90-tonne-glw, 66-tonne-capacity EVA bogie tanks (E.862) were also briefly seen in the caustic-soda traffic from Seal Sands, including ICA 33 80 7994 003-1, photographed at Tees Yard in November 1998. However, they proved unsatisfactory and shortly thereafter were returned to the Continent amidst rumours of barrel fractures. *Mark Saunders*

Below: To replace the EVA tanks Dow leased, five 90-tonne-glw, 69-tonne-capacity ICAs (E.842), from GE Rail Services, and this type proved rather more successful, also taking over the caustic-soda traffic that ran from Immingham and Runcorn. No 33 87 7797 037-1 was photographed weekending in Tees Yard in March 2000.

Below: Simotra tanks also worked to the North East, one batch being engaged in hexamethylenediamine traffic from France to the ICI nylon plant at Wilton, while from 1989 a pool of three Simotra tanks (33 87 7996 037/046/047) carried propanol from Tees Storage at Middlesbrough Dock Hill, the Local Working Instructions having been amended to allow them to enter Tees Storage despite their having a higher (*i.e.* more restrictive) Route Availability rating than was normally permitted over the bridge that gave access to the terminal. Built by CFMF in 1981 to diagram E.516, ICA 33 87 7996 037-0 was photographed at Tees Yard *en route* to the train ferry in August 1991.

15. MORE TWO-AXLE FERRY TANKS

Left: Enoxy Chemical, previously the International Synthetic Rubber Co, was located at Hardley Siding, near Hythe, just north of Esso's Fawley oil refinery, from where it drew much of its feedstock. However, certain hydroperoxide chemicals arrived by rail from Germany for use as epoxidising agents for curing the polyester resins and elastomers produced at the works. Loaded with p-menthane hydroperoxide, ICX 21 80 0780 352-9 was recorded at Hythe in August 1979. Built in 1963, it measured 7.5m over headstocks and had a 4.5m wheelbase. Assigned diagram E.234, it had a gross laden weight of 32 tonnes and could carry a payload of 21.5 tonnes. *Trevor Mann*

Right: Similar in size but rated at 40 tonnes glw and with a carrying capacity of 29 tonnes, ICB 2380 7391 016-4 (diagram E.302), loaded with diisopropylbenzene hydroperoxide for Enoxy, is seen at Dover in October 1986.

Left: Loaded with p-menthane hydroperoxide at Dover in 1986 is ICB 23 80 7398 400-3, the single 40-tonne tank to diagram E.371. Built by Graaff in 1971, it measured 8.46m over headstocks and had a 6m wheelbase. Unfortunately rail traffic to Enoxy Chemical ended in 1991.

Right: Two-axle Etra SA Swiss-registered ferry tanks occasionally came to Britain with chemicals for the Ciba-Geigy pharmaceuticals plant at Grimsby and its agrochemicals works at Whittlesford. Built by J. Meyer in 1979, ICB 23 85 7398 502-1 was spotted at Immingham *en route* to Grimsby West Marsh in September 1986. Measuring 8.81m over headstocks, and with a 5.4m wheelbase, it was one of a batch of 22 tanks assigned diagram E.493. Although its orange Kemler-style hazard-warning panel displayed UN substance-identification number 1993, denoting 'Flammable liquids, non-toxic', closer inspection of the wagon label revealed it to be loaded with propylbromodioxolan.

Below right: Another rare find, ICB 21 80 0085 709-2 was one of nine 40-tonne hydrogen-peroxide tanks built by Franz Kaminski in 1970 for German chemical company Elektrochemische Werke. Allocated diagram E.340, it measured 7.5m over headstocks, had a 4.5m wheelbase and could carry 30 tonnes. When spotted at Warrington Central in August 1978 it was on hire to Peroxid-Chemie, a subsidiary of Laporte. Hydrogen peroxide is used widely in bleaches and disinfectants, and Laporte was one of the world's leading producers, but it made limited use of rail once the Warrington plant lost its own private siding in 1970. *Trevor Mann*

Below: Loaded with sodium-chlorate solution (a bleach used in the production of paper), Simotra 35-tonne tank 21 87 07892 078-1 is pictured at Ipswich in April 1979 while *en route* from Harwich to the Wiggins Teape mill at Corpach. Unusually for a ferry wagon it was unfitted but had both air and vacuum through pipes, making it an ICR on TOPS. Assigned diagram E.347, it measured 7.1m over headstocks, had a 4m wheelbase and could carry 24.3 tonnes. *Trevor Mann*

16. PHOSPHORUS TANKS

Left: In 1988 the Albright & Wilson works at Langley Green, Oldbury, began receiving regular deliveries of molten phosphorus from Roosendaal, in the southern Netherlands. Initially VTG tank wagons were used, but as the traffic increased 10 EVA 80-tonne phosphorus tanks were built by Graaff in 1989, among them ICA 33 80 7996 008-8, found in Washwood Heath Yard in October 1995. Allocated diagram E.718, it measured 13.22m over headstocks and could carry 55 tonnes.

Below: Seen being shunted towards the train ferry at Dover in April 1995, ICA 33 80 7996 106-0 was one of another batch of ten 80-tonne phosphorus tanks, introduced by OnRail in 1991. The phosphorus was used in the manufacture of flame-retardant and water-treatment compounds, and Langley Green handled three or four wagons a week until the train ferry ceased, the last discharged phosphorus tank returning to the Continent on Thursday 21 December 1995, a day before the final sailing.

17. STAINLESS-STEEL TIPHOOK TANKS

Right: Among the wagon types introduced by Tiphook in 1987 were a batch of 40 air-braked 90-tonne stainless-steel bogie tanks (E.686). Built by Arbel Fauvet, they measured 17.66m over headstocks, had a 62.7-tonne payload and, being fitted with 100mm glass-wool insulation and steam-heated outlets, were suitable for a range of commodities. In 1989 three of these bogie tanks replaced a pool of five British Petroleum 45-tonne two-axle tanks carrying acrylonitrile from Immingham Dock Acid Plant to the BP Chemicals works at Barry Docks, and TIA 33 70 7899 039-3 was photographed in this traffic at Immingham in October 1990.

Below right: In 1994 twenty of the Tiphook bogie tanks were sold to Nacco, renumbered under French registration as 33 87 7994 010-029 and reassigned to diagram E.698. Four were then leased to Cerestar for a new international working between its factory at Trafford Park, Manchester, and plants in France. This involved the tanks' running loaded in both directions, carrying different grades of Corn Steep Liquor (CSL), but this efficient two-way operation, conveying 10,000 tonnes of CSL a year, ended in October 1995 when corporate changes within Cerestar resulted in the cessation of all the company's rail flows between Britain and the Continent. No 33 87 7994 018-2 is seen at Trafford Park soon after the traffic started, in May 1994.

Below: Following the demise of the Cerestar traffic 33 87 7994 018-2 was amongst four ICAs to be hired by ICI to transport caustic soda from Sandbach and Runcorn to the Roche works at Dalry and British Nuclear Fuels' reprocessing plant at Sellafield. Repainted in ICI livery, it was recorded at Warrington in July 2001.

18. CHALK AND CHINA-CLAY SLURRY TANKS

Left: Chalk and china-clay slurry for use by the paper, board and pottery industries have long constituted an important rail traffic, with points of origin in Britain and the Continent. Between 1984 and 1986 Franz Kaminski and Link Hoffmann Busch built sixteen 80-tonne bogie slurry tanks (E.554) for VTG. British-registered, they measured 13.16m over headstocks and had a payload of 58 tonnes. Working from the English China Clay works at Quidhampton, near Salisbury, to customers in Aberdeen and at Corpach and Port Elphinstone, they were a common sight on the West Coast main line and could also be seen carrying chalk slurry from Belgium to Sittingbourne via the train ferry. TIA 33 70 7895 163-5 passes through Warrington Bank Quay in April 1987.

Below: The VTG tanks were fitted with lagged and sloping barrels to prevent the slurry from freezing and to assist in unloading, and these features were incorporated on the 120 90-tonne slurry tanks built by Arbel Fauvet in 1989 (E.719). Numbered 33 87 7898 000-119, the batch was split between Locatransport (000-039), Nacco (040-079, 100-119) and Oeva (080-099). The majority of the Nacco-owned tanks were used on internal slurry flows from Quidhampton and Burngullow, while those belonging to Locatransport and Oeva worked from Vise, north of Liège. Beneath a threatening sky Locatransport's ICA 33 87 7898 027-0 waits to leave Longport in April 1999.

Above: After ECC opened a new depot at Stoke Cliff Vale in 1982 clay traffic ceased to be handled at Longport, but the sidings were still used to marshal local freight in the Stoke area. The new depot normally received seven or eight slurry tanks each week, and several are awaiting unloading in this view recorded at Cliff Vale in March 1999.

Below: Measuring 13.22m over headstocks, the E.719 diagram tank seemed to fill the viewfinder nicely. A work-stained 33 87 7898 098-1 is pictured at Stoke in October 1999.

Above: At Workington the slurry tanks were unloaded at the docks, from where a road tanker made the final delivery to the Iggesund board mill. Here 33 87 7898 054-4 was being unloaded in May 2005.

Below: In 2007 the Nacco tanks were renumbered under German registration and used for a new block working between Belgium and Irvine. Here 37 80 7898 119-8 passes through Warrington in June 2008.

Right: When traffic increased in the 1990s 64 former Ermewa bogie wine tank wagons were lagged for use on various slurry flows. The majority were operated by ECC out of Burngullow, Quidhampton and Vise, but Norwegian company Omya leased 20 to convey imported chalk and marble slurry from the Croxton & Garry terminal at Aberdeen Waterloo to Blackburn, Corpach, Sittingbourne and Workington. Loaded with slurry for the Sappi paper mill, 33 87 7890 548-3, an ICB to diagram E.446, is pictured at Blackburn in December 1997.

Above: Amongst the British-registered ferry wagons in slurry traffic were five TIA bogie tanks built by Fauvet Girel for STS in 1987. All measured 14m over headstocks, the first four (E.680), built on underframes recovered from withdrawn LPG tanks STS 78650-53, having a gross laden weight of 80 tonnes and a carrying capacity of 58 tonnes, while the fifth (E.688), using the underframe from former Class A tank STS 86000, was a 90-tonner with a 68-tonne payload. All five worked initially for ECC from Burngullow and Vise before being transferred in 1997 to the Croxton & Garry / Omya pool. No 83 70 7895 203 -8 is seen at Aberdeen in July 1992.

Left: Unfortunately the blue livery faded badly, as evident from this shot of the single 90-tonner, 83 70 7895 204-6, at Stoke in September 1996.

Above and below: These two photographs of the famous 'Silver Bullets' also illustrate the effects of more than 10 years' intensive service. This batch of 27 90-tonne slurry tanks, built in 1989 in France by ANF Industrie to diagram E.708 for Tiger Rail, worked from Burngullow to the Caledonian Paper mill at Irvine and remained so employed after acquisition by Nacco in 1992. Contrast the condition of TIA 33 70 7890 124-2 at Coalville Open Day in June 1989 with that of 33 70 7890 120-0 at Crewe in February 2000.

19. WINE AND GLUCOSE TANKS

Left: Ermefer SA of Geneva operated a pool of more than 120 tank wagons leased from Ermewa and Fert & Co to carry wine, spirits and fruit juices from France to customers throughout Europe. In Britain their most important destination was London International Freight Terminal, but there were also regular deliveries to Telford Bottling at Wellington and Saccone & Speed at Aylesbury as well as seasonal traffic to Manchester IFT, Newhaven and Stafford. The bottling plant at Aylesbury usually handled two or three bogie tanks a week, but one morning in May 1985 ICB 23 87 7390 501-9 was noted arriving in the local trip freight from Bletchley. One of five 36-tonne wine tanks built by Ateliers de Joigny for Ermewa in 1970 to diagram E.360, it measured 7.1m over headstocks, had a 4.5m wheelbase and held 4,410 gallons.

Left: Nine batches of 80-tonne bogie wine tanks were built by Fauvet Girel and CFMF between 1974 and 1982. Most numerous were the 45 tanks built by Fauvet Girel to diagram E.446, which included ICB 33 87 7890 591-3, photographed at Dover on 17 October 1989. They measured 13.46m over headstocks and held 12,000 gallons.

Below: Somewhat shorter, at 12.49m over headstocks, ICB 33 87 7890 601-0, built by CFMF to diagram E.440 for Fert, was also photographed at Dover that same day.

Above: In 1982 Fauvet Girel built seven dual-braked and lagged wine tanks for Ermewa (E.539), among them ICX 33 87 7899 008-9, spotted at Aylesbury in June 1985.

Below: Aylesbury was also the main destination for the three dual-braked 80-tonne wine tanks (E.530) owned by R. W. Armstrong. Built by CFMF in 1982, they measured 14.93m over headstocks, held almost 13,000 gallons and worked from Slovenia (then a part of Yugoslavia) until the traffic ceased in 1989. No 33 87 7899 002-2 is pictured at Aylesbury in 1985.

Above and right: Photographed at Warrington in February 2002, ICA 33 87 7990 001-2 was one of three specially equipped 80-tonne tanks assigned to diagram E.891 and used to carry liquid sugar from France to the Roche factory at Dalry, where it was used in the production of Vitamin C. To maintain the load at a constant temperature the wagon was fitted with an on-board heating plant.

20. GOING NUCLEAR

Left: In addition to handling spent fuel from British nuclear power stations the BNFL works at Sellafield reprocessed fuel from overseas reactors. Spent fuel from Japan arrived by sea at Barrow Docks, from where the flasks were carried up the Cumbrian Coast to Sellafield, and between 1977 and 1982 BREL's Ashford Works built BNFL nine large well wagons for this traffic. Each measured 24m over headstocks and was mounted on two pairs of Y25C bogies, the first six (E.474) capable of carrying 101 tonnes, while the last three (E.529) were strengthened and could handle up to 116 tonnes. Last of the fleet, KYA 33 70 9986 008-8 arrives at Sellafield with an NTL11 81-tonne flask in June 2005.

Above: Until 1995 Nuclear Transport Ltd also operated a number of eight-axle nuclear flask wagons conveying spent fuel to Sellafield, in this case via the train ferry from power stations in Italy, Switzerland and the Netherlands. Most numerous of the NTL types were the eight French-registered 105-tonne-capacity vehicles built by Fauvet Girel between 1977 and 1981 to diagram E.475. Fitted with two-piece sliding flask covers, they measured 19.46m over headstocks and ran via both Harwich and Dover. IQB 33 87 9985 003-1 is shunted in Dover Town Yard in June 1994.

Left: NTL also operated two 90-tonne-capacity flask wagons (E.697), built in 1989 by Waggon Union, which were used to carry irradiated fuel from the German light-water reactors at Gundremmingen and Unterweser. The first of the pair, IQA 33 80 9987 000-2, stands outside the THORP building at Sellafield in October 1993. *David Ratcliffe collection*

21. CAR-CARRIERS

Right: Historically, internationally registered car-carriers have been few in number, it being more economic, having carried new cars to the port by rail, to drive them onto a Ro-Ro ferry and leave the wagons behind. However, in 1958 BR introduced 40 two-axle 20-tonne Carfit C wagons for ferry service. Built at Ashford Works, they measured 33ft over headstocks, with a 22ft 6in wheelbase, and had very low sides and drop-down ends. Initially vacuum-braked, they were fitted with air brakes *c*1961 and later acquired UIC numbers in the range 21 70 4140 000-039. Assigned diagram E.212, they carried military vehicles such as Land Rovers and small armoured cars, but by the early 1980s most were being used as barrier wagons for block oil trains. FIX B 748143 (21 70 4140 033-4) is seen at Ellesmere Port, performing just such a role in February 1982. *Trevor Mann*

Above: In 1993, as plans for Channel Tunnel freight services took shape, STVA introduced a fleet of 350 double-deck four-axle car-carriers to diagram E.791, including IPA 23 87 4392 513-9, seen passing Didcot in July 1994 at the rear of a block train carrying new cars from the Rover plants at Cowley and Longbridge *en route* to Arluno in northern Italy.

Right: Problems of vandalism and theft soon resulted in the fitting of side-screens. No 23 87 4392 717-6, reassigned to diagram E.792, is pictured at Cowley in March 1997.

Above: For the Rover traffic STVA also leased, from Tiphook, a fleet of 56 three-axle articulated double-deck Autic wagons (E.735). Built by SNAV in 1979, they were 25.76m long, had a carrying capacity of 12 tonnes and were renumbered for international duty in 1993. PIA 43 70 4288 033-0 (previously numbered RLS 92010/11) was recorded at Washwood Heath in October 1995.

Below and above right: Gefco's fleet of 150 IPA four-axle double-deck wagons (E.742) was introduced in 1996 to supply its distribution depot at Corby, the bulk of the traffic comprising Peugeots and Citroëns from France. The top deck of 23 87 4392 093-2 had already been unloaded when this photograph was taken at Corby in July 1997. Note that, in order to maximise capacity within the limited headroom of the lower deck, one car is facing in the opposite direction from all the others.

Right: Providing the ultimate in protection from both the stone-thrower and the car-radio thief were 60 fully enclosed car-carriers introduced by Auto Care Europe in 1994. Built by Arbel Fauvet to diagram E.789 and coded WIA, each wagon was 66.36m long and comprised five elements carried on two outer and four inner articulated small-wheel Y39 bogies. The roof and body sides, which were made of an aluminium composite sandwich, were lifted vertically by electrically controlled jacks to facilitate access to the top deck, while, unlike conventional car-carriers, both floors were virtually flat to speed up loading and unloading. When new a few WIAs were adorned with Ford and ACE logos, among them 85 70 4971 007-5, spotted at Tees Yard in February 1999.

Left: The logos were removed as the wagons moved between pools operating on behalf of Mazda, Nissan and Rover in addition to Ford. No 85 70 4971 044-8 waits to be loaded with imported Mazdas at Queenborough in April 2000. *Trevor Mann*

Above and left: Eighty-two 22.5-tonne single-deck four-axle wagons (E.825) designed to carry commercial vehicles were introduced by STVA in 1995. In these photographs IPA 43 87 4333 072-4, loaded with Land Rovers and Range Rovers for Italy, passes Didcot in April 1997, while 43 87 4333 012-0, carrying a Ford Scorpio estate, a Courier van and two Transit chassis, waits to leave Dagenham in October 1996.

22. TIPHOOK 'PIGGYBACKS'

Right and below right: Although the type has long been popular on the Continent, the restrictions of the British loading-gauge meant that 'piggyback' wagons capable of carrying road trailers were not seen on BR metals until 1990, when Tiphook purchased 100 from the Finnish wagon-builder Rautaruuki. Allocated diagram E.736, they measured 15m over headstocks, could carry a 37-tonne payload and ran on Y27SS1 bogies. Leased by Charterail, the majority were used in petfood traffic from Melton Mowbray to Cricklewood, although they also appeared in freight service between Glasgow, Warrington and London. The wagons' central section swung out for a road trailer to be reversed onto the deck, then returned to its original position and locked into place for transit. One fine morning in September 1991 KOA 83 70 4798 057-3 was being loaded at Melton Mowbray, while 83 70 4798 014-4 was ready to leave.

Left: The collapse of Charterail resulted in these innovative wagons' going into store, and although 83 70 4798 048-2 was briefly used to transport a milk tanker from Penrith, where it is seen in July 1997, nothing came of this trial, and they were eventually withdrawn. *Mark Saunders*

Above and below: In 1979 Franz Kaminski built three 40-tonne two-axle container flats for Schering AG, an associate of ICI, to carry aluminium alkyl halides from Germany. The wagons (E.501) measured 10m over headstocks, had a 6.6m wheelbase and could carry either two or three individual demountable tanks or up to nine smaller tanks mounted within container frames. In addition to working to the ICI plant at Wilton they occasionally ran to BP Chemicals at Grangemouth. Prior to the introduction of the purpose-built IPAs this traffic, which was used in the polymerisation of ethylene, had been transported in two-axle lows, but, irrespective of the wagons employed, barrier vehicles were required either side of the load. Nos 43 80 4141 500-3 and 43 80 4141 501-1 were photographed at Wilton on the same day in September 1988. *Trevor Mann (both)*

Above: Rather more numerous were the 300 40-tonne flats built by
Transfesa in 1994 (E.735) to carry swapbodies containing automotive
components between the Ford plants at Valencia (Spain) and Dagenham,
although ride-quality problems restricted them to 45mph.
IFA 24 87 4438 055-6 is pictured at Dagenham in October 1996.

Below: Photographed at Warrington in January 1990, IFA
31 87 4572 229-4 was one of a batch of 21 56-tonne SNCF Multifrets
introduced in 1989. Leased to Freightliner, they worked initially from
Harwich Container Terminal to others around the country before being
added to the general Railfreight Distribution / SNCF container-wagon
pool in 1993.

Left and below left: Also in 1993 Arbel Fauvet and Remafer began the construction of more than 500 pairs of permanently-coupled bogie flats, and although there were a number of detail differences between batches each pair could carry either two 40ft or four 20ft containers — or, in the case of swapbodies, two 13.6m or four 7.82m, or a combination thereof. Known as 'Euro-Twins', they were intended primarily for Channel Tunnel traffic but also saw extensive use on domestic freight flows within Britain. When new the Euro-Twins were painted in various colours including black, green, grey, purple and blue, depending on the hirer, but within a few years they had all taken on the same grubby appearance. Railfreight Distribution's FIA 31 70 4938 125-2 (E.790) was recorded at Deansgate station with a stack of Flatrack containers from Trafford Park in June 2000, while Remafer-built IFA 33 87 4909 140-5 (E.834), carrying two 30ft powder containers, was photographed passing the same spot in August 1998.

Right: Categorised by owner AAE, a Zurich-based operator of Continental vans and container flats as '104 Megafret Multiloaders', these permanently coupled low-deck twin-set wagons were introduced in 1999. With a loading platform only 825mm above the railhead, they could accommodate 9ft 6in-high containers up to 45ft long and had a total payload of 89 tonnes. The first sets were seen in Channel Tunnel services, but subsequently many have been leased by EWS, DRS and Freightliner for use within Britain. When spotted in July 2000 at Ipswich Griffen Wharf IFA 33 68 4909 762-9 (E.861) was carrying two 20ft boxes loaded with imported spirits.